The Student's Guide to Life

Essential lessons on love, learning and success

Andrew K. J. Tan

Aktive Learning
10 Anson Road #21-02
International Plaza
Singapore 079903

E-mail: publisher@aktive.com.sg
Online book store: http://www.aktive.com.sg

ISBN 981-05-6973-4

National Library Board Singapore Cataloguing in Publication Data

Tan, Andrew K. J., 1980-
    The student's guide to life : essential lessons on love, learning and
        success / Andrew K.J. Tan. – Singapore : Aktive Learning, 2007.
    p. cm.
    ISBN : 981-05-6973-4 (pbk.)

    1. Youth – Life skills guides. 2. Youth – Conduct of life.
    3. Interpersonal relations in adolescence. 4. Study skills. I.
Title.

HQ796
646.700835 – dc22
SLS2006046552

Printed in Singapore

Dedicated to my mother

CONTENTS

PART ONE: Growing Up

PART TWO: Family Feuds

PART THREE: Making Friends

PART FOUR: That Special Someone

PART FIVE: Schoolhouse Rock!

PART SIX: A Life Worth Living

PREFACE

I was nineteen when I started work on this book, twenty when I finished. I submitted the manuscript to a local publisher, who wrote back suggesting I make some changes and resubmit. I never did. Publishing is an act of hubris where the author tells the reader: "I have written something worthy of your time and effort." And I thought to myself: *Who am I to tell others how to live?*

So I put the manuscript aside and got on with life, spending four wonderful years at Stanford University plus two more in the working world. I had forgotten about the manuscript, but one day chanced upon it, and flipping through the dusty pages realised there was much of value within. The keys to who I had become and what I had achieved in the intervening years were largely in there. And at twenty-seven more confident/arrogant (only a fine line between the two), decided to publish and share it with you.

I am mindful the title promises much and I intend to deliver the best I can. But while I have attempted to be comprehensive and to substantiate my views with research and personal experience, this book is not an encyclopaedic treatise covering everything from Shakespeare to STDs. Treat it more like an older brother giving advice to a younger sibling – sometimes opinionated, sometimes blunt, but always meaning well.

Getting a book from prose to print is a Herculean task. I could not have done it without the contributions of my friends Ann and Belle, who always knew I was a chronic procrastinator, but probably did not expect this book to take eight years. Kudos to my designer Leng and Yap Teck Koon of Linographic Services, for patiently working with me and doing excellent work. As for Linli, her professional portrait photography made me feel like a model. And finally to Han Xu, for her legal eagle eyes and endless encouragement that made all the difference.

I have edited for brevity and updated some examples to make them easier to relate to, but the manuscript remains substantially in its original form. I hope what I have written is worthy of your time and effort.

Yours,

Andrew K. J. Tan

April 2007

READ THE INTRODUCTION

This is the book I wish I had when I was thirteen.

I wish I knew what I know now about how to manage my time, how to make lifelong friends, and the importance of pursuing my interests. Instead I wasted much time in meaningless activities in the name of "fun". Now that time is gone forever. But the nice thing about life is, as long as you're alive you have more time.

Have you ever felt:

- ✦ "I avoid looking at myself in the mirror. I hate the pimples on my face, the shape of my body, the way I move."
- ✦ "I quarrel with my parents all the time. They just can't stop nagging and lecturing me."
- ✦ "I wish I had more friends. When I get back from school everyday, I ache from the loneliness."
- ✦ "I have to get a boyfriend/girlfriend somehow. It's like you're inferior or something if you don't have one."
- ✦ "There's so much pressure on me to do well. I know I'm supposed to study hard and do my homework, but I've got no motivation to do these things."
- ✦ "I don't know what I want to do with my life. I've got no ambition or goals. There's nothing I'm interested in. I'm just drifting along."

I know I have. And I've heard friends and peers express the same feelings countless times. And I remember wishing for something or someone we could consult to alleviate the angst of being a teenager and a student.

> The mass of men lead lives of quiet desperation.
> – *Henry David Thoreau*

If you want to take control of your life and steer it towards a destination of your choice, this book is for you. You will get relevant information to help you understand and deal with real-life situations. You will also find encouragement and inspiration.

Growing up is tough. Sometimes we all need a bit of help to get us through a sticky situation. This book was written to provide that.

An experiment

Let's try an experiment. Find a clock near you, and look at it for three minutes. During these three minutes, I want you to i) keep your eyes on it, ii) focus your thoughts on it and iii) feel enthusiastic about the task. Do not read any further until you are done. Begin now.

Did you do it? Chances are you didn't try at all. It was a boring experiment and you didn't see the point. If you did try it, were you able to keep your eyes on the clock for the full three minutes? Did you manage to think of nothing but the clock? Could you feel enthusiastic about the task?

What you would have noticed is as long as you *wanted* you could keep your eyes on the clock. Your eyes are under your conscious control. But you probably found it tougher to keep your thoughts solely on the clock. Maybe your thoughts drifted to what you'd be having for dinner or to your barbeque with your friends this weekend, or to what guys supposedly think about every forty-seven seconds (soccer, that is. What were you thinking about?). Feeling enthusiastic about the task was the toughest thing to do. What's so interesting about a clock?

What's the lesson here? You have much conscious control over your actions as compared to your thoughts or feelings. As long as you want to do something, your body will obey as best as it can. Your thoughts are harder to control – they flit in and out of your head, and it takes a lot of effort to focus them on something. Your emotions are largely beyond your conscious control, but your thoughts and actions can affect them.

Think back to a time when you completed a school project, perfected a difficult song on your guitar or succeeded in getting a date with someone you were attracted to. You felt groovy. And unless you're a hopeless pessimist, your thoughts about it were positive too – "I did great!" or "I have a chance!"

The action came first, and then the thoughts and feelings followed. If your actions led to a successful result, positive thoughts and feelings followed. You can do it the other way too – rev up your thoughts and feelings to inspire yourself to act. There's no right or wrong way – feelings, thoughts and actions are inextricably linked.

In this book you will learn to take an action-oriented approach to life. This book is not a fluffy, feel good, "Just think positive!" kind of book. It is full of practical advice and real life observations that will jolt your thinking and prod you to re-examine your approach to life.

Your thoughts are important, but you must act on the right ones. Figure out what you want to do, how to do it, then do it. You don't always have to feel like doing it. In many cases, once you get started on something, you'll feel a whole lot better about it.

In a cinch:

Self-awareness + Know-how + Action = Lasting positive change

That's the last formula you'll see in this book, I promise.

What good can a book do?

But, you might ask, what good can a book do? A book is only a stack of paper with words printed on it. If you read it and consider the author's message you might gain some knowledge or a deeper understanding. But knowing how to do something is different from actually doing it. There comes a point when you have to take action to realise a desired result, and that is completely up to you.

Deep down everyone knows this. It's common sense. But just being vaguely aware of it, being able to relate it to your reality, and doing something to improve your situation are all very different things.

This book will not make a difference in your life if you don't DO anything about it. It's hard work to break out of your old habits of acting, thinking and feeling and to acquire new ones. But it can be done. When you take control of your habits, you take control of your life.

This book is divided into six parts of five chapters each, together thoroughly covering a student's main concerns:

PART ONE: Growing Up covers the emotional and social changes you experience through your teenage years. It is also about the importance of making good use of your time.

PART TWO: Family Feuds provides insight and assistance into your often tenuous relationships with parents and siblings.

PART THREE: Making Friends is your guide to getting along with people and building lifelong friendships.

PART FOUR: That Special Someone explores the nature of romantic love, from attraction to rejection.

PART FIVE: Schoolhouse Rock! delves into the purpose and importance of getting an education, and provides you with tips on making the most of your schooling experience.

PART SIX: A Life Worth Living takes a bird's eye view of the different facets of your life, and gives you a system to help you set goals and manage your time so you can have more fun and achieve more at the same time.

Who am I to write this book?

I am not an expert on life. Just like you, I'm stumbling and fumbling my way through, but a little further down the road, and I have one redeeming quality – I like to learn.

For years, I have been reading what people much wiser than myself have to say about leading life in a fulfilling and productive way. When I tried to apply their teachings to my life, some ideas worked and some didn't. Some were too simplistic, others didn't make sense. This book contains the ideas, tips and methods that worked for me.

Let's begin!

Part 1
Growing Up

Brief Contents

THE END

I stood at the base of her coffin, petrified. I was afraid to see the expressionless face of someone I once knew. Would her face be bloated, garish, bluish-purple? I didn't want to know. I turned around and left. I was, and still am, afraid of death.

She was a schoolmate of mine back in school. I didn't know her well, but she always had a warm smile for me whenever we met along the corridors. She was an accomplished gymnast and debater, a radiant person. Then I stopped seeing her along the corridors. I later found out she had leukaemia. She fought the disease bravely, but eventually succumbed.

Young people die. From recent memory I recall reading about a student being knocked down by a bus. Another schoolmate of mine died while backpacking in China.

I'm not trying to scare you. There's no need to be paranoid. I fully intend to live to a ripe old age and I hope you do too. But we also have to acknowledge the fact that accidents and tragedies do happen, and just because we're young doesn't make us immune or invulnerable or immortal.

Life is fragile. It's scary to think about it, and most of us block the thought when it enters our mind, but we will all die someday and we don't know when. It could be tomorrow or a hundred years later.

And it's difficult to talk about death with your friends or parents because it's so taboo. People don't want to think or talk about it. But it is natural to have such thoughts and feelings and they need to be addressed.

When I finally admitted the possibility I could die anytime, it gave me a sense of urgency in the way I led my life. I asked myself: How am I going to spend the time I have left, especially when I don't know how much more I have? If I were to die tomorrow, would I die with no regrets? Would I be proud of the life I led so far?

Sometimes we come across movies or inspirational quotes telling us to lead every day as though it were our last. That doesn't make sense to me. If today were my last day, I wouldn't bother about the future. I'd spend all my money, do all sorts of dangerous things or spend the whole day crying. It didn't make sense to live everyday like that, because in reality life could go on for a long, long time. Yet it also doesn't make sense to live life in preparation for some distant future ("When I retire I'll finally do what I really want to do ...") as we might die anytime.

So I came to the conclusion that the best approach is to strike a balance between enjoying life one day at a time and living for the future. It's a paradox – to live like you are going to die tomorrow and in a hundred years at the same time. But there is truth in paradox. Light cannot logically be a particle and a wave at the same time. But it is.

It is uncomfortable and most of us avoid thinking about death, especially our own. But if we waited till we had to it would be too late. Wouldn't it be terrible to have so many regrets and unfulfilled dreams you had no time to address?

Spend a minute to consider how you would lead your life with the end in mind. What would your friends and family say about you? Would they miss you dearly and keep your memory alive in their minds?

Thinking about death has given me a new perspective on life. Most things – how I did on a test, losing a possession, being insulted – are insignificant when you take such a perspective. Be careful about focusing too much on trivial and unimportant things and losing sight of the things that really matter in your life – your family, your friends, your contribution to this world.

There is no time but now

Have you ever been asked: "What is the time?"

All you had to do was glance at your watch and read off the time. But what if you were asked: "What is time?" How would you answer that?

How do we tell time? By looking at a watch or clock and identifying the hours, minutes and seconds. "Clock time" is certainly useful – it gives us a standard measurement of the progress of a day so we can structure our activities. But it doesn't tell us what time is.

Is time the spinning of the Earth on its axis (each rotation takes about twenty-four hours)? The rotation of the planets around the sun (Earth takes about 365¼ days to complete one orbit)? The movement of the Universe from its creation (or the Big Bang depending on your beliefs) to Armageddon?

Some people believe time is an absolute reality, like a big clock in the sky ticking away relentlessly regardless of what we think, feel or do about it. Albert Einstein gave us a different view of time by thinking of it as a dimension in addition to the three dimensions of space (length, breadth and depth). Time is relative, so depending on how fast you're going it can seem to speed up or slow down. Einstein came up with the Theory of Relativity by imagining himself riding a beam of light to the ends of the universe. Imagine that!

> Imagination is more important than knowledge.
> – *Albert Einstein*

Whether you think time is absolute or relative, there is no time but now. What's past is set in stone behind us – we can't go back to change it. What's ahead is murky and unknowable – we can't accurately predict it. The only time we have is now. Our past choices determine who we currently are. And the choices we make now will shape who we are in the future.

I like to think by making good choices on how we spend it, we are able to extract the essence of time, or what I call "time juice". By making the effort to choose and apply our lives in meaningful and productive ways, we can reap the rewards and squeeze a little more of this "time juice" into our cups. Of course, it's not the quantity but the quality of the juice that matters – how sweet and nourishing it is. Thinking this way also gives me licence to make corny statements like: If life gives you a lemon, squeeze it.

Have you ever felt regret for things you should have done – studied harder, treated your friends better or put more effort into learning a new skill or sport? You might feel it's too late now.

But it's *not* too late. You still have *now*. What are you going to do *now*? And how will you look back on this point of time in the future – with satisfaction or with regret?

In the film *Dead Poets Society*, a new English professor played by Robin Williams brings his class to look at faded black-and-white photos of old boys of the school pinned up at the trophy corner. "We are food for worms, lads," he says to his class as they stare intently at the photos. "Believe it or not, each and every one of us in this room is one day going to stop breathing, turn cold and die." He asks them to listen closely to the photos for the legacy of those who have passed on, and as the boys lean in to listen, the professor whispers in their ears, "Car-pe...car-pe...carpe diem. Seize the day, boys! Make your lives extraordinary!"

Preparing for the journey ahead

We'll be exploring many issues and I'll be sharing my personal views as well as ideas from experts in various fields. You don't have to agree with everything you read, but keep an open mind. As you discover new ways of looking at things, ask yourself these questions:

- ✦ Does this make sense to me?
- ✦ Can I relate my experiences to this?
- ✦ How can I apply this to improve my life?

The essence of adolescence is about testing boundaries, challenging authority and developing your own views and ideas. Words by themselves are lifeless, mere splotches of ink on paper. Only you can breathe life into these words by engaging with the ideas they represent.

FROM KID TO ADULT

During the carefree days of childhood your parents were usually there to take care of your problems. But as you transition into adolescence there seem to be more things to worry about and nobody to help you.

It's sometimes hard to have a balanced view of life when you're buried under so many problems. You're down, the future looks bleak and everyone around you seems unfriendly. Help's on the way – in the coming chapters you will learn strategies to help you deal with your problems. Life is full of obstacles, and you will enjoy a deep satisfaction from engaging and overcoming them.

The ABCDs of Growing Up

What does it mean to "grow up"? I found an answer in Dr. M. Scott Peck's book *The Road Less Travelled*. I was twelve when my form teacher Ms. Faviola Fernandez recommended it to my class. But it was only three years later when I saw the book in a library that I decided to read it. *The Road Less Travelled* is one of the most challenging and eye-opening books I have ever read, and I highly recommend it.

Dr. Peck uses the following as conditions for mental health, which are representative of the qualities we ought to have as mature human beings:

1) *Accepting Responsibility*
Life is tough. Are you going to resign yourself to fate, or are you going to take action to improve your situation? Accepting responsibility is not about gaining control over other people, but about being accountable for your life.

> I am the master of my fate:
> I am the captain of my soul.
> — *William Ernest Henley, "Invictus"*

Do not blame circumstances, external agents or other people for your life situation. If I blame McDonald's for making me fat, then that is a lot of outlets I have to raze to the ground in a cholesterol-induced arson attack. And even if I manage to raze them all, nothing will have changed but the target of my blame (KFC anyone?).

2) *Balance*
For life to be successful and fulfilling there has to be balance – between work and play, between solitude and sociability, between responsibility and freedom.

Think about how you divide your time between your studies, extra-curricular activities, hobbies, friends, family and the development of your self. Which areas are you spending too little time on?

3) *Conscious Living*
Living consciously means to not hide from problems you are aware of, to not relegate them to your subconscious mind. Pay attention to yourself. Be aware of the dialogue going on in your head. Learn about what motivates you, and what triggers you to act in a certain way.

Take smoking as an example. Smokers tend to associate certain times and rituals of the day to puffing on a cigarette. Start work, smoke. Coffee break, smoke. Finish lunch, smoke. Addiction is not just physical but also psychological, borne of habit. The behaviour is so habitual the smoker is no longer conscious of it.

4) *Delaying Gratification*
The greatest barrier to leading a fulfilling and productive life is your desire for instant gratification. People want love, results, satisfaction, and they want it *now*. Washboard abs in five days. A girlfriend or boyfriend via a chat line in five hours. Happiness in five minutes.

Every moment of your life you are faced with a choice: Are you going to spend your time on an activity that will give you short-term pleasure or will you invest your time and effort in a long-term goal? Are you going to do your homework or watch TV tonight?

> Delaying gratification is a process of scheduling the pain and pleasure of life in such a way as to enhance the pleasure by meeting and experiencing the pain first and getting it over with. It is the only decent way to live.
>
> – *M. Scott Peck, The Road Less Travelled*

To avoid the discomfort of this effort, most people procrastinate and do the easy thing. If there is something you have to do anyway, to me a better philosophy is to "suffer first, enjoy later" rather than vice versa. Once you have suffered, you can enjoy yourself without guilt and anxiety about the "trials" ahead.

If you accept responsibility for your life, balance your expenditure of time so no significant facet of your life is neglected, live consciously and delay gratification for longer term benefits, you will approach Dr. Peck's idea of "mental health".

This will take time. Becoming a mature person is a marathon, not a hundred-meter sprint.

THE MOUSE IN THE MIRROR

Self-esteem – your regard for yourself – determines your effectiveness at meeting the challenges life throws you, be it a tennis ball or a two-ton wrecking ball. Of course, if you get hit by a two-ton wrecking ball not even your self-esteem can save you.

Constantly belittling and doubting oneself is a common problem, and if you have this habit, you need to develop psychological skills to counteract it. Some signs of a poor self-image:

+ **Feeling inferior.** You are afraid to make eye contact with people because you fear being found unworthy. Your speech and body language is nervous.
+ **Always apologizing.** You apologise before you say or do something, even if the other person is in the wrong.
+ **Fear of failure.** You are afraid to try new things or to make mistakes.
+ **Conformity.** You would rather act like everyone else than assert your own individuality.
+ **Rejecting compliments.** You downplay or refuse to accept praise, admiration or congratulations from others.

Step by tiny step

What can you do to become more confident and self-assured? Some people are resigned to the "fact" that they are worthless or incapable, believing there is nothing they can do about it. There are undoubtedly things largely outside of your control – the weather, freak accidents and other people being some of the obvious examples. But there are also things largely within your control – your behaviour, your attitude and your words. One effective approach is to control what you can and accept what you cannot.

> God grant me the serenity to accept the things I cannot change, the courage to change the things I can, and the wisdom to know the difference.
>
> – *The Serenity Prayer*

What you think of yourself has drastic implications for every aspect of your life – your work, your relationships and your achievements. Some actions to start your journey towards a healthier self-concept include:

✦ **Learn to be conscious of what you say to yourself, how you feel and what you do as a result.** We speak to ourselves all the time. Try to catch the thoughts and feelings that led you to take a certain action, or that resulted from an action.

✦ **Distance yourself from people or situations that diminish you.** You need to remove yourself from as many negative influences as possible, as it is easy to return to your old ways of thinking and behaving.

✦ **Develop your performance confidence.** Gain proficiency in a skill or hobby you enjoy, one small step at a time.

✦ **Focus on helping others.** Often by serving others we lose a large part of our self-consciousness and our "self-ishness".

✦ **Push yourself to continually take risks outside of your comfort zone – the boundaries of thought and action within which you feel safe.** Examples of this include talking to people you do not know, or trying out a new activity. By doing this you will find your comfort zone slowly expanding, and you become less and less afraid of unfamiliar situations, and more and more confident in your ability to face new ones.

✦ **Learn from people you respect and admire, who represent to you a model of healthy self-esteem.** How do they talk, move and do things? How do they relate to people and handle tricky situations? You may wish to emulate them, or "fake it till you make it" – pretending to be the kind of person you want to be until you really become that person.

✦ **Regularly evaluate yourself in a constructive way and look for ways to improve.** Criticise your specific actions and not your entire self (e.g. "I should have read the instructions before I pushed the red button and started a global nuclear war" instead of "I'm such an idiot").

The lifelong climb

Building up a solid sense of self-worth is a long-term process. Do not be discouraged if you see little improvement initially. As long as you continually push yourself in the direction you want to go, you will make progress.

When I was thirteen, a good friend of mine invited a group of girls to go for an outing but did not invite me. Instead, he asked this other friend who was socially confident. I felt hurt. My friend explained his decision by telling me he thought I was too shy and would clam up and not talk at all, creating an awkward situation. He did not say this out of malice but out of a kind frankness. And he was right. This intensified my belief that I was a "shy" and "uninteresting" person (you see what you want to see).

Now as I look back on this event many years later, I realise I've changed in a marked and noticeable way. I am more confident of myself and more able to express myself. I've been taking small steps in pushing the boundaries of my comfort zone in new situations or with new people. I am keen to try new experiences that are not physically dangerous, and am less nervous about talking to strangers.

> Mind the pattern. A pattern of mistakes is a call to change your life. The rest of the tapestry is not determined by what has been woven before. The weaver herself, blessed with knowledge and with freedom, can change – if not the material she must work with – the design of what comes next.
> – *Martin Seligman, "What you can change ... And what you can't"*

Only action will break you out of the negative downward spiral of "disbelief-inaction-greater disbelief". Building a solid self-esteem may seem a tough and frustrating process, but if you don't start now, then when? The destination is distant but the journey is well worth it.

BEING RESPONSIBLE

As an adolescent you may feel stuck in a limbo between childhood and adulthood – you are given some of the responsibilities of an adult but are treated like a child.

You may find that adults (your parents, teachers and others you come into contact with) do not hold your opinions and ideas in high regard. You may have an ingenious idea for a more efficient way of doing something or even for a new business, but you'll often run straight into a brick wall when you try to communicate these ideas to them.

They say things like "you don't know what you're talking about", "you're too young and inexperienced" or "you don't know what the real world is like." These disparaging remarks can deal a heavy blow to your confidence.

Let's be realistic – adults are in charge. They run and own everything – families, businesses and the government. Without your parents' support you are unlikely to survive on your own. The cost of renting even a single room is likely to wipe out much of what you'll earn by taking a job that requires no qualifications.

The best strategy to gaining their trust, respect and serious consideration is not to be more rebellious and defiant, but instead to be more adult-like – mature, responsible and professional in your dealings with people.

This doesn't mean you have to become boring or stuffy. You are fully entitled to go out and have fun and enjoy yourself as much as you can, as long as you know what you are doing.

You may be ostracised by some of your peers for taking such a "radical" attitude; many will not be able to see the consequences of their actions beyond the lure of a short-term thrill or "kick". Learn to look beyond the opinions and attitudes of your peer group. There are more than six billion people on this planet. The people you hang out with form the minutest percentage of this ever-growing total, and there are people out there who are completely different.

Seek out friends of like mind – people you can discuss serious ideas with without fear of ridicule. Better still, find an adult mentor (it could be a teacher or an adult you respect) to guide you. This could save you much wasted effort and frustration as you make your entry into the world of adults.

Taking personal responsibility

In order to have control over your life, you must take personal responsibility for it. You cannot blame circumstances or look for scapegoats.

In his book *Taking Responsibility*, Dr. Nathaniel Branden writes about the importance of self-responsibility and self-reliance in the development of a healthy individual. You have some basic choices – to live consciously and responsibly or unconsciously and irresponsibly – that have a decisive influence on the quality of your life.

You are free to choose your path. This freedom of choice is both your greatest gift and heaviest burden, as well as what makes you human. It can be a source of joy and personal power if you make the best and highest choices. There is an intimate relationship between your success and happiness and the amount of responsibility you take for choosing goals and values to live by.

The world is changing rapidly. With the advent of the Knowledge Economy your mind is becoming your most valuable asset. To be successful in the working world of the future, you have to proactively solve problems and seek out new opportunities instead of passively waiting for someone to tell you what to do. You must think critically and be creative and innovative at the same time. You need to be able to learn continuously and to manage your time properly.

And the best time to develop all these critical skills is now, while you are still in school. You have the time, teachers to guide you and a relatively risk-free environment to experiment in. Take responsibility for what you are learning both inside and outside of school by choosing to spend time to equip yourself with the skills and knowledge you need for the future.

Your areas of responsibility

It is sometimes scary to think about how soon you will be entering the real world and (hopefully) becoming a productive member of society. You will have to support yourself or even a family and have all sorts of obligations to meet.

You may worry about your ability to handle adult life and its entailing responsibilities. Being responsible means making rational and moral choices as you are answerable for your behaviour.

Your current areas of responsibility include:

✦ **Personal.** You have to treat yourself with respect and develop a healthy self-esteem.

✦ **Family.** As a son or daughter to your parents, and a brother or sister to your siblings, you have to behave and obey the family rules.

✦ **School.** As a student you are expected to attend classes regularly, to be punctual for school, obey the school rules and to actively participate in class. You also have to do your homework, study for your tests and respect your teachers and fellow students.

✦ **Social.** You are responsible for choosing your friends and the company you keep, and are accountable for how much you let your peers influence your actions and the situations you get yourself in.

✦ **Financial.** You have to learn to budget by limiting spending and saving up for things you want to buy.

✦ **Legal.** You are responsible for keeping on the right side of the law. Ignorance is not a valid defence in court. Breaking the law can land you in more trouble than you're able to imagine.

All this talk about responsibility can be a drag. You want to enjoy life and not be bogged down by these things. I fully agree that life should be fun and exciting, but true freedom is not gained by abandoning your responsibilities.

It is the opposite. By being responsible you will gain control over how you lead your life instead of having to constantly react to the problems and crises that erupt when you shirk your responsibilities. Life is far more enjoyable that way.

ME? GENIUS?

> Know thyself.
> – *Inscription on the Oracle of Apollo at Delphi, Greece*

Continual insight into your self is the basis for a thoughtful life. An understanding of your own nature, abilities and limitations will give you a keener grasp of the world and help you make wiser decisions.

"Ah, but of course I know myself. I spend so much time with me!" you say. Do you truly know who you are? Your strengths? Your weaknesses? Your passions? Your values? The major goals in your life?

If a stranger stops you in the street and asks you: "Who are you, really?" you're likely to give him a strange look and hurry away. But suppose you decide to humour him and answer his question. What would you say?

Most people would say something like this: "My name is Brad. I'm a student, and I'm fifteen years old." Pressed for more he might add: "I play tennis for my school and I have two sisters." If you're telling someone you met in a chat room about yourself, you might also tack on some physical description: "I'm tall, dark and people say I look like Brad Pitt."

You are likely to define yourself in terms of your name, occupation, age, interests, family background and physical characteristics.

But is that it? Is that who you really are? Surely someone who has the same name, age, number of siblings and height as you is not you. What else do we have to consider to get at the essence of the true you?

- ✦ **Your talents.** Everyone has different talents, areas he or she is particularly gifted in. Maybe your gift is in music or sports, or in solving puzzles.
- ✦ **Your strengths and weaknesses.** What positive and negative qualities do you have? Are you self-disciplined, compassionate and courageous? Dishonest, impatient and irresponsible?
- ✦ **Your outlook on life.** Are you an optimist or a pessimist? When bad things happen to you, do you blame yourself or others?

✦ **Your aspirations and ambitions.** Do you know what your goals and dreams are? If you did not have to worry about making a living or the opinion of your parents and peers, what would you do with your life?

✦ **Your values.** What principles or purposes do you believe are worthwhile? Which is most important to you: freedom, self-expression, wealth, fame, power, making a difference or helping others?

✦ **Your habits.** What are your habits – of speaking, eating, studying, relating, moving, thinking? Examine your life closely to spot these recurrent, often unconscious patterns of behaviour.

"Whoa, boa," you say, "you mean I'm supposed to know all these things? How is that possible?" You will not figure these things out in a day, but keep asking yourself these questions and observing the way you think, speak and act. The answers will slowly filter through to you.

You're smarter than you think

Of all the opinions people have of themselves, one of the most damaging is: "I'm stupid." Perhaps they started thinking of themselves in that way after doing poorly on a test, or after they compared themselves to a "smarter" person. Parents, teachers and friends often make such hurtful comparisons as well.

What is intelligence anyway? Who is smarter – a science whiz or a talented guitar player? One student might do better than another in the classroom, but much worse out in the soccer field. If you are lost up in the mountains, who would you rather have with you – a math genius or an experienced trekker?

If we define intelligence as the ability to handle new situations successfully and the capacity to learn from one's past experiences to improve future performance, then intelligence does not just depend on your IQ score but on the context.

This is borne out by studies done in America on the predictive value of IQ tests, i.e. the relationship between a person's IQ and his future level of success. These studies found that IQ scores are excellent predictors of school success but not real world success.

IQ tests measure "schoolhouse giftedness". Real world intelligence includes a much broader range of skills. Harvard psychologist Professor Howard Gardner came up with the term "multiple intelligences" to describe the repertoire of skills and abilities that can be found in every walk of life. The eight categories of intelligences identified by him are:

- **Linguistic.** The ability to work with words to argue, persuade and entertain. Proficiency in reading, writing and speaking, perhaps in more than one language.
- **Logical-mathematical.** The ability to work with numbers and logic to solve problems. You use this intelligence to reason, to analyse patterns and sequences, and to think rationally.
- **Spatial.** The ability to work with pictures and images; to visualise and to draw; to have a sense of depth and space; to be able to work mentally in three dimensions.
- **Musical.** The ability to perceive, appreciate and produce rhythms and melodies. People who are strong in this aspect have a good ear for music, can keep time, sing in tune, and may have perfect pitch.
- **Bodily-kinesthetic.** The ability to control movements and to manipulate objects skilfully. A person who is strong in this area is hands-on, has good tactile sensitivity and is physically active.
- **Interpersonal.** The ability to understand and work with people and to perceive their moods, intentions and desires. Competence in relating and forming bonds with people.
- **Intrapersonal.** The ability to probe the inner self – one's feelings, emotions, thoughts and desires.
- **Naturalistic.** The ability to recognise flora and fauna, to use the natural world productively. Biologists, farmers and environmentalists are strong in this area.

With an understanding of the concept of multiple intelligences, we can see how someone who brands himself "stupid" because he is relatively weaker in his linguistic or logical-mathematical intelligences has denigrated his own potential and his abilities in other areas. With the concept of multiple intelligences we can identify and value a broader spectrum of human talent and abilities.

You may recognise your strength in one or more of the eight intelligences, but you possess all of them. You are relatively stronger in certain areas and weaker in others, but you can improve every area.

Unleashing your genius

Develop your abilities in all eight intelligences. You do not need to be a master in every area, but working to improve all the areas is a way to reach your potential. Developing intelligences you are strong in will help you excel. Developing intelligences you are weak in will add an extra dimension to your life and bolster your confidence in this new area of competence. In other words: Bank on your strengths and bankroll your weaknesses.

Take an inventory of your relative competency in the various intelligences. As an example, my own assessment is as follows:

- ✦ **Linguistic: Strong.** I can write and speak well. I enjoy reading and working with words.
- ✦ **Logical-Mathematical: Quite strong.** I didn't have many problems with Mathematics in school although I am not brilliant in this area. I can reason and think rationally.
- ✦ **Spatial: Quite weak.** I find it difficult to visualise images and to work mentally with three-dimensional objects. I'm not good at drawing.
- ✦ **Bodily-kinesthetic: Quite weak.** I've never been a very active or athletic person. My movements are clumsy and uncoordinated.
- ✦ **Musical: Quite weak.** I tried learning to play the guitar before but never really got anywhere. I find it difficult to sing in tune.
- ✦ **Interpersonal: Quite strong.** I may not be the most popular guy around but I do have a few good friends. I can relate to people and I'm usually friendly.
- ✦ **Intrapersonal: Strong.** I think a lot about life, who I am and what I want to be. I enjoy my solitude and can have a good time when I go out alone.

✦ **Naturalistic: Quite weak.** I do not know much about nature in general. I do, however, enjoy being in natural environments like forests and hills.

Once you have profiled your strengths and weaknesses, choose which intelligences you want to start working on, then formulate a plan to help you improve. The following are examples of activities you can do to strengthen each intelligence:

Linguistic
✦ Read more newspapers, magazines and books
✦ Learn a foreign language
✦ Join a public speaking course or club, e.g. Toastmasters International

Logical-mathematical
✦ Work on logic puzzles or brain teasers for fun
✦ Learn a programming language
✦ Do calculations mentally instead of using a calculator
✦ Read a book or take a course on critical thinking
✦ Teach or tutor someone else in science or mathematics

Spatial
✦ Work on a jigsaw puzzle
✦ Take up photography
✦ Learn drawing, painting or cartooning
✦ Learn to use a graphic design software on your computer
✦ Practice visualizing things in your mind

Bodily-kinesthetic
✦ Take up a physical activity like swimming, tennis or basketball
✦ Exercise regularly
✦ Learn a craft where you'll have to work with your hands, e.g. woodcarving or sewing
✦ Practice yoga or meditation
✦ Take dance lessons

Musical
- ✦ Attend concerts and performances and pay attention to the individual voices or instruments
- ✦ Join a choir, band, ensemble or a cappella group
- ✦ Take vocal lessons
- ✦ Learn to play a musical instrument

Interpersonal
- ✦ Keep in touch with your friends regularly
- ✦ Volunteer for school or community programs
- ✦ Take up a leadership position in your student group or club
- ✦ Talk to someone you meet regularly but have never spoken to

Intrapersonal
- ✦ Keep a journal to record your thoughts and feelings on the day's events
- ✦ Spend fifteen minutes every week to think about where your life is going and what you've done
- ✦ Read inspirational and self-improvement books
- ✦ Take a personality test to discover your strengths and weaknesses
- ✦ Write a poem to express yourself

Naturalistic
- ✦ Take a walk in the park and notice the different kinds of trees and plants
- ✦ Climb a hill
- ✦ Visit the zoo and learn about the animals there
- ✦ Keep a pet or try growing plants

There are many more things you can do – the point is to start valuing the different skills and abilities you have. You are not permanently handicapped in any particular area; it just depends on how much effort you put to work on your weaker areas. By developing each of your different intelligences, you enrich your life.

Part 2
Family Feuds

Brief Contents

TAKING OFF FROM THE NEST

There comes a time in life when you must learn to stand on your own two feet. Becoming an adult means you have to establish a separate identity apart from your family. You want to be your own man or woman and do your thing. You strive for independence and freedom, but often undermine a credible claim to it by being irresponsible and immature. "I don't care," you wail, "I just want to do it my way! Waaaaa!"

But your freedom and independence has to be *earned*. By keeping the consequences of your actions in mind and making reasonable and rational choices, you begin to establish credibility with your parents. Breaking all the rules your parents set down just because they are rules, without any thought to whether those rules are beneficial or not, is irresponsible.

Demonstrate your maturity by thinking through those rules. Follow those that make sense and negotiate those you feel are unreasonable. For example, parents often forbid their children to stay overnight at their friends' places. Rather than throwing a tantrum or running away from home because you want to attend a friend's overnight party, explain clearly and truthfully to your parents what you'll be doing there and with whom, and provide contact numbers for them to reach you. Assure them you are able to make sensible choices and stay away from trouble. You'd better be, or they'll never buy this line again.

If you act responsibly, you will earn their trust and respect, and eventually the freedom you crave. Freedom is not about being free of curfews, restrictions or inhibitions. It is about balancing your pursuit of life's opportunities with the self-control to act responsibly. Keep in mind the consequences of your choices – you are responsible for them.

Of course, it's possible that after your best efforts at being diplomatic and reasonable you get a flat-out "NO!" from your parents. Well, all that goes to show is that they're the ones who are unreasonable.

Your adolescence can be a time of rapidly escalating levels of conflict with your parents. Sometimes you find you're just quarrelling all the time without really knowing what you're quarrelling about. Sounds dumb, but it happens. Dumber still is stubbornly doing what your parents don't want you to do instead of what you want to do. It might sound cool to be a "rebel without a cause", but rebellion just for the sake of rebellion can only lead to senseless bloodshed and a miserable family life.

How rebellious you are also depends heavily on what sort of disciplinarians (doesn't that word send a shudder down your spine?) your parents are. Some parents are unbearable dictators, where even the slightest sign of disobedience leads to severe punishment. Some teenagers resign themselves to a lifetime of slavery, and carry around an imaginary ball-and-chain of parental control over them well into their adult lives.

On the other extreme, some parents operate a laissez faire style of discipline, where anything goes. "You're running off to Thailand with a man twice your age whom you met on the Internet yesterday, dear? Do have fun, and here's some cash for the trip." A total lack of a disciplinary structure in your life imposed by your parents signifies indifference on their part to you ("They don't love or care about me").

Parental rules and regulations, though often restrictive and annoying, demonstrate their concern for your safety and well being. You don't want to be tied down by your parents, but you want to know they care.

In between is the happy mean of enough parental discipline to let you know they care and to keep you out of trouble, and enough freedom to let you explore your identity and learn to be independent.

They're still your parents after all

You have a part to play, however, in ensuring this period of your life is one that does not do permanent damage to your relationship with your parents. You need your personal space to develop a unique identity, and dominating parents can be a stumbling block. Thus you might find you have no choice but to distance yourself from them for a while. Take the time to explore and establish who you really are and to build up strong friendships outside of your family, but do not sever ties with your parents. Make time for family activities and maintain at least a minimal level of contact. Once you have reached adulthood and are more secure in your own identity, you will have the confidence to grow closer to your parents.

PLAYING PING-PONG WITH YOUR PARENTS

If you have a great relationship with your parents, go give them a hug and skip right to the next chapter. If not, what irks you about your parents? Probably one or more of these:

- **They try to control your life.** Your parents force you to do things they think are "best for you" without any regard to what you think. They might give you the illusion of choice, but it is Hobson's choice. In other words, you've no say at all.

- **They invade your privacy.** Parents who eavesdrop on your telephone conversations, scan your email or read through your diaries are infringing on your privacy. It is impossible to trust parents who do these things as they show little trust in you.

- **They nag you endlessly.** "You should…", "You ought to…", "How come you're not…", "Don't ever think of…", "Don't be…". Day in, day out, they reprimand you on every aspect of your life, from the types of friends you should be making to how long you've not cleaned your room. I had a friend whose mom shouted at him all day long. We'd be talking on the phone and in the background you could hear his mom screaming at him to do his homework or to take care of some chores. This lasted our entire conversation, and he just tuned her out.

- **They jump to conclusions.** Your parents return home and see you sitting on the couch watching TV and say, "You lazy bum! You've been watching TV all day and obviously haven't done your homework." They have pronounced you guilty without a fair trial. This parental trait is one of the most repugnant, especially if you did do your homework and extra review on top of it. They do not believe you can be up to any good without their watchful supervision.

Can we talk?

Can you change your parents? I don't think you can change anybody but yourself. You can try talking to them about your concerns, but only they can decide if they want to do something about it.

Even so, it's up to you to make the effort to have the best possible relationship with your parents. Your natural reaction may be to hit back at anyone who tries to control your life, who nags you endlessly or who accuses you of things you have not done. But this will not resolve the underlying problem. Try acting differently:

+ **Tell them how you feel.** Instead of putting the blame on them by saying, "All my friends' parents let them go for this camp, why won't you?", try "I'd feel left out if all my friends got to go for this camp and I didn't." Use the word "I" instead of "you" when voicing your complaints. They will get to hear your side of the story instead of being put on the defensive. They cannot deny how you feel, and this is likely to get better results than plain old mud slinging.

+ **Tell them specifically what you want.** Be reasonable and as specific as you can. Ask for an hour's extension to your curfew, or permission to attend a night art course instead of demanding "more freedom". Decide what is most important to you, then ask for it.

+ **Offer something in exchange.** You could offer to sweep the floor or wash the dishes in exchange for the privilege of going for a friend's party or to stay out later on weekday nights.

Of course, after all's been said and done, your parents could still refuse to grant you any concessions. Many parents get upset if their children try to bargain with them. "Do as you're told!" they roar. Maybe after doing all you can you realise you can't seem to get along with your parents at all. Take heart that this situation will not last forever. Meanwhile, you could:

+ **Confide in a friend.** Tell a friend you trust about your problems. If your friend is in a similar situation, you can take comfort that there are others who are going through the same thing as you. They might also offer constructive insights into your problem.

✦ **Don't antagonise them.** Stay away from potentially antagonizing situations with your parents, especially if you know they're in a bad mood. For example, if your dad always comes home from work grumpy, you can stay in your room and wait till the storm clears before approaching him for any matter.

✦ **Concentrate on the parts of life you enjoy.** It could be reading or school, or a sport you're good at. Focusing your energy on an activity you enjoy will distract you from problems with your parents, and give you less time to mope around at home.

Letter from the Institute of Adolescent Advancement

If you're looking for a quick fix to your parental problems, give yourself a hard bop on the head (haven't you learnt anything about delaying gratification?). However, if you're desperate and are willing to discharge me from any liability, try sending the following letter to your parents:

Dear Parent,

We are writing to share with you the findings of the latest scientific research carried out by the Institute of Adolescent Advancement. We strongly urge you to pay attention to the findings and make the necessary changes in your interactions with your adolescent. Failure to do so statistically predisposes your adolescent to depression, acts of violence and suicidal tendencies. You wouldn't want to take that chance, would you?

Times have changed. Do not try to run your children's lives. Our studies have consistently shown that over-controlling parents lead to frustrated children with low self-esteem. We know you want the best for your children, but sometimes the best thing to do is to let them make their own decisions.

Adolescents have been found to possess extremely short attention spans. Their conscious minds are unable to register the significance of anecdotes longer than three sentences. Be concise and to the point. Do not nag – you are most likely wasting your breath.

Instead, learn to listen attentively to your adolescent. It is a crime to jump to unsubstantiated conclusions. Doing this will effectively shut down all channels of communication.

Respect your adolescent's privacy. Do not go through their things, read their personal letters or diaries, interrogate their friends, listen in to their phone calls or hire a private investigator to tail them. If they find out, your trust quotient will immediately be reduced to zero. A loss of trust is a major predicting factor of rebellious behaviour.

Aim to understand your teenager in today's context. Your standards may be outdated, and relying on them will lead to fundamental miscommunication. Of course, do not take this to an extreme by mimicking their behaviour, or they will die of embarrassment. They expect you to act like parents.

Finally, a point that cannot be overemphasised. The continuing existence of inflation in our country has led to an increase in the cost of living, and a reduction in the purchasing power of your child's allowance. For example, if we take the current annual rate of inflation to be 7.2% (a rough figure, plus or minus 7.2%), then the cost of a Big Mac will double every ten years. That means that in fifty years time, it will have increased by more than thirty-two times! We thus recommend an across the board increase of allowances by a hundred to two hundred percentage points, in order to help your child take advantage of the current lower prices.

Thank you.

Yours Faithfully,

Andrew K. J. Tan

Director, Institute of Adolescent Advancement

Seal the envelope, affix a stamp, send it off, and it's only a matter of time before you'll see "tangible results". Meanwhile, cast off your shackles of subjugation and shout "I want to break free!" in the privacy of your own room where no parent can hear you.

DEALING WITH SIBLING RIVALRY

Born and bred under the same roof, siblings not only share similar genes but also spend a large chunk of their lives together. This gives them the time to develop a lasting bond if things go well, or to irritate the heck out of each other.

I remember when I was a little runt and my brother and I wrestled to settle our disagreements about who should be using the computer. There was one small problem – my brother was twice my size. At the time, we had what you would call a love-hate relationship. He loved to pin me to the ground until I surrendered, and I hated every moment of it. Like the average older sibling, though, my brother did exhibit protective behaviour towards me. Whenever I learnt a new swear word he would be the first to scold me, and if I didn't listen to him, it was back to Wrestlemania.

The roots of sibling rivalry

Siblings have to compete for the limited resources available in any household, foremost of which is the time and attention of their parents.

Everyone wants to be loved and valued by their parents, and the presence of one or more siblings means you have extra competition for your parents' favour. Sore points for comparison include your academic and sporting achievements, intelligence, social skills and level of maturity.

A younger sibling who has an accomplished older sibling will be judged by those standards, and may feel like he is constantly living in the shadow of his older sibling. If he is unable to meet his older sibling's standards of achievement, he may be branded inferior.

An older sibling who has a brilliant younger sibling, on the other hand, will naturally feel a sense of jealousy towards this "young upstart" who has wrested favourable attention away.

Quarrels can also originate from interference in your life by your siblings – an invasion of your privacy, mistreating of your friends or "borrowing" your property without telling you all constitute hot spots for tempers to flare up.

Declaring a truce

To maintain a workable peace, take the initiative to make positive changes in the way you deal with your siblings, without first requiring them to treat you nicely. Often only an agreement to stop quarrelling and start discussing who uses what, and who does what and when is needed as the first step towards establishing more harmonious relationships with your siblings. Remember to:

✦ **Treat your siblings like your friends.** If at all possible, you'd try to be reasonable and upbeat when resolving disputes with your friends. Do the same with your siblings, and always look out for the possibility of cooperation and sharing to diffuse your disagreements. This includes being honest with them about what you want and what you are willing to give up, and then sticking to your agreement afterwards.

✦ **Respect their rights.** Your brother or sister has as much right to watch a certain television program over the one you want to watch, or to use the phone or computer as you do. Granted, there are occasions when you need to use these things to carry out productive work while your sibling just wants to engage in idle chatter or to burn time. But generally speaking, if you want them to let you use something at a particular time, you have to make concessions to let them use it at another time.

✦ **Respect their privacy.** Your siblings have the right to their own private lives. Do not insist they share every part of their lives with you, and do not lose their trust by going through their things or eavesdropping on their conversations.

Overcoming the jealousy you feel towards a sibling involves discovering your own unique talents and recognizing your worth as a human being. There is little point in constant comparison; it is not about winning or losing. What is the point of proving your superiority to your sibling?

ALTERNATIVE FAMILIES

The standard idea of a family is a social group which consists of a man, a woman and their 2.1 biological kids. There are, however, a large variety of alternatives.

There are single-parent families, single-child families, stepfamilies and families with adopted children. All these groups consist of two or more people who have long-term commitments to each other and who usually live under the same roof, who provide companionship and security for their members. However, many of these "deviant" families are not looked kindly upon by society.

Single-parent families and stepfamilies are a result of the rising rates of divorce and separation. These types of "broken" families are seen in a harsh light because it is thought that they cannot provide their children with a nurturing environment and proper role models.

The later average age of marriage and financial burden of having a child have also led to a decrease in the rates of childbirth and an increasing prevalence in the number of single-child families.

If you belong to any of these "less-than-ideal" families, you might feel deprived of a proper family experience. I don't belong to an "ideal" family either, and in my opinion the quality of your family is far more important than it having the standard components of a man, a woman and 2.1 kids.

There are still opportunities in these "less-than-ideal" families for you to grow and develop into a thoughtful and loving individual. In fact, you are likely to become independent and mature before your peers. We will now examine two of the more common types of "less-than-ideal" families – single-parent and single-child families.

The all-in-one parent

Single-parent families have an obvious disadvantage – there are less resources and parental attention available for the children. The lone parent most likely has to work harder to support the family on a single income, and this means mom or dad has less time to spend with and less money to spend on the kids.

Children living in single-parent families will also lack a male or female role model in their lives. But then again, it is better to have no role model at all than to have a negative one – an abusive and irresponsible parent will do more damage if he or she is around. Having one quality parent around is better than having two constantly quarrelling ones.

If you're in a single-parent family, be understanding to your parent. Not only does he or she have to balance a career with the work of raising kids, but also has to deal with the stress and complications of being a single parent. That's tough, and your parent might be prone to flaring up or breaking down at the slightest provocation. Keep these outbursts in perspective.

Do also get involved in the decision making process in the family, as your parent could sure do with another mature view or opinion. If you're the older sibling in the family, you'll have to take extra care of your younger siblings. Take it as a learning experience, and take heart knowing you're growing to be a responsible person.

Going solo

Being an only-child was traditionally thought to be a disadvantage by some psychologists. The child is deprived of valuable learning experiences from his siblings, such as the sharing of toys or learning to speak. It was felt the only-child's capacity for cooperation, intellectual development and socialization was compromised.

The unfettered attention and concern of parents towards an only-child was also thought to encourage dependency, timidity and selfishness. Being an only-child was not a good situation to be in.

But more recent studies reveal that only-children do not differ from other children in their levels of anxiety or misbehaviour. They have actually been found to be more independent and self-reliant than other children.

These studies also show only-children prefer solitary activities as compared to group ones, and have less need to be liked and accepted by their peers. But their peers do not find them any less sociable and they are not lonelier than other children. They have learnt to enjoy solitude, and yet successfully garner their need for emotional support and companionship from their social network as well.

The results from these studies jibe with my experience. My only-child friends are generally well adjusted and sociable. They are able to enjoy themselves when they're alone and do not constantly crave companionship. There's a huge difference between being alone and being lonely.

If you're an only-child, your friends probably play a large role in your life. If you put more effort into cultivating your friendships, you are likely to have more rewarding friendships. You're also likely to have a better relationship with your parents as they're more attentive towards you. They also have more financial resources and time to spend on you, so enjoy it while you can!

PARENTING AND SEX...EDUCATION

The family is the fundamental unit of society. Ideally, it should meet the basic needs of its members, namely the need for food, shelter, clothing, security and love.

If your family was unable to provide you with those things when you were growing up, you had a tough start on life. But every calamity you survive only makes you stronger. We respect people with disadvantaged backgrounds who become successful in life, for their tenacity and strength of will to overcome the obstacles they faced. Their drive was strengthened by the trials they underwent; their ambition stoked by the poverty (whether material or otherwise) and suffering they experienced.

There is no point feeling envious of someone else's "lucky" situation or feeling angry at your having been short-changed by life. All of us have lessons we need to learn in our lifetime, and some people get a more challenging syllabus.

Parenting anyone?

> All happy families resemble one another, but each unhappy family is unhappy in its own way.
> – *Leo Tolstoy, Russian novelist and philosopher*

Put yourself in your parents' shoes for a moment – you have a bunch of rude, rebellious and inconsiderate kids who are constantly quarrelling with their siblings. You come home from work exhausted everyday and the only thing you want is some peace. Instead those ingrates come up to you demanding extra cash to go watch a concert or to buy new clothes they'd only wear once anyway.

You cannot understand how the prices of things have rocketed since you were a teenager. How can going out for a movie be *that* expensive? If only those brats knew how difficult money was to earn, how you bled and sweat for every dollar they now happily pour down the drain. Some days you feel as though nobody would notice if you just installed an

ATM in the house and hung a sign that read "MOM" ("Money Offering Machine") on it.

It's tough to be a parent. Parents have their own needs – for privacy, leisure and some space of their own. And yet they have to meet the needs of their children as well.

If your parents are going through a difficult period – maybe because of financial worries or relationship problems – they may give you a tough time too. They might be edgy and quick to scold or punish you, sometimes for no apparent reason at all. It'll be an unpleasant period to live through but do know it's less about you than about the situation. Most parents try to do a good job. Don't make it tough on them and on yourself as well.

You need to be a mature and responsible adult before you can become a good parent. That's why teen pregnancy is a big no-no – it is cruel to bring an infant into this world without having adequate ability and sufficient resources to bring it up properly. And thus the importance of proper sex education.

Erm, well, you see ... it's about the birds and the bees

Isn't it amazing how one of the most fascinating subjects can be turned into a boring class lecture with some poorly drawn diagrams and a hemming and hawing teacher who constantly has to clear her throat?

It's no wonder that most of us turn to our friends, books or the Internet to find out more about sex. Surveys show parents as the source the least number of teenagers turn to. It's too awkward for most parents to bring up.

Other than by carrying out campaigns there is little the government can do to force parents to teach their kids about it, though it won't hurt to encourage them to do so. Then again it might do harm as kids and parents across the country start dying of sheer embarrassment.

Including it as part of the school syllabus is one way to ensure every young person knows something factually accurate about sex. And it needs to be done early, maybe for primary school kids between the ages of ten and twelve, or it may be too late for some. Some might feel it is too early to teach this subject in primary school – with knowledge may come temptation. But to me that is better than a life ruined by ignorance.

More needs to be done to address the emotional aspects of this sensitive issue. The technical aspects are usually well covered, but lack the needed impact and resonance in the mind of a young person. You don't just want the facts and the figures or a list of Dos and Don'ts.

When I was eleven my primary school decided to give us a comprehensive grounding in this important area. So we got to watch the standard "gross and yucky" videos, which were less educational than sensational ("Did you see that? Eeeww yeuch!").

But on top of that, we also had a free and easy discussion session with our form teacher Mr. Ong, a teacher anyone would be glad to have. I remember Mr. Ong reassuring a classmate that it was perfectly normal for boys our age to discharge a teaspoonful's worth of sticky white liquid during the night. "Phew," my classmate sighed, relieved he was not lagging behind the current production targets for the average adolescent male.

The most memorable lesson I learnt during those sessions was, however, of a somewhat different nature. Having been married for a while, Mr. Ong knew what he was talking about when he shared this nugget: Women have a far greater capacity for pleasure than men do.

Now isn't that the kind of thing you'd want to learn as compared to the boring genitalia-related bits you already know everything about? We were only eleven, but felt like the wisest know-it-alls who had not even spoken to a girl before (I was from an all-boys school).

Amazingly, I had almost no sex education in secondary school. If you were unable to receive an excellent sex education, fret not. Go read up on what you want to know. Books usually contain more reliable advice than what you find out from your friends. If you use the Internet there will be a lot more pictures but I cannot vouch for the quality of the information. Oh, and do not use the school computer to do your "research".

As long as you are unsure about the physical and emotional ramifications of having sex, take this piece of advice: Don't do it.

Part 3
Making Friends

Brief Contents

THE LONELINESS DISEASE

Once I was talking to my friend Mel about the evils of acne: "Acne destroys a teenager's self-image. When I get a huge pimple, I can't stand looking at myself in the mirror. I feel so ugly."

But acne is controllable – there is salicylic acid and benzoyl peroxide for the mild cases, and antibiotics and retinoic acid formulas are available for even the most serious cases. If the beginning stages of acne are identified promptly, pre-emptive measures can be taken to prevent much of the scarring that haunts many unfortunate teenagers.

Being concerned about acne is not being vain. Acne is a skin disease. If you had a fungus growing on your foot, you would not hesitate to get some anti-fungal cream to eliminate it. There is nothing wrong about seeking treatment for acne.

"More should be done in schools to screen for this. Think of how much unnecessary suffering in silence that could prevent," I said.

"More should be done about loneliness too," Mel said.

"But loneliness can't be cured!"

Or can it?

Acne is a disease of civilization. Tribes living in isolation do not suffer from it. In a closely-knit tribal society, loneliness probably does not exist either, and can be thought of as a disease of civilization too.

Loneliness is a negative mental and emotional state characterised by feelings of isolation and a lack of meaningful relationships with others. Loneliness is distressing. It is like living in a psychological and emotional desert. Most of us know what it is like to be in a crowd but yet to feel lonely. Even though people surround us, we know they don't notice or care about us.

We do many things to escape loneliness. We might turn on the television, listen to CDs, read a book or watch a movie by ourselves. But the relief these things provide is superficial.

Are you lonesome tonight?

How closely these statements reflect your experience will give you an idea of how lonely you are:

- ✦ I don't feel connected with the people around me.
- ✦ No one knows the real me.
- ✦ I can't find companionship when I need it.

Loneliness can be transient. If you're at party where you do not know anybody except the person who invited you, you'd most likely feel lonely for a while till you make some new friends. This sort of loneliness is situational, and most of us feel it from time to time. It is a normal reaction to being put in a context where you are temporarily unable to connect with the people around you.

More damaging is chronic loneliness. This persistent form of loneliness has become a habitual way of life. You feel there are few people you can share your thoughts with. You are unable to discuss ideas or perceptions you have with the people around you. You cannot find enjoyable companionship for activities like having dinner or watching a movie.

Being alone is different from being lonely. You can be alone but not feel lonely. All of us need time for ourselves to rest, to think and to reflect – we need time for solitude. Some of us enjoy taking part in solitary activities like writing poems or stories, painting or reading. These are positive experiences we partake in to nurture ourselves. Enjoying your solitude is a very different experience from the gnaw of loneliness.

Overcoming loneliness

Loneliness is a state of mind rather than something that has happened to you, and you can take steps to shed your feelings of isolation and alienation.

Meeting people is a necessary first step to feeling connected again. If you put in the initial effort to meet more people you will experience a virtuous cycle – you meet more interesting people; you feel better about meeting people; it gets easier to meet even more people.

So where do you meet new people? Explore the obvious avenues first. The people you regularly come into contact with are prime candidates for your initial attempts. These could be the familiar faces you see at school, the bus-stop or the library every day. Especially at school, there are hundreds if not thousands of people out there you could get to know, and it is up to you to go and meet more people.

Places where you find people with similar interests are also a good bet. These could be a student group or sport, or even classes and hobby clubs. There, you are expected to mix around and to introduce yourself, taking a lot of the stress away. Take part in activities that interest you, whether it be swing dance, hiking or chess. By doing so you will share at least one thing in common with everyone – your interest in the activity. This is a common bond you can use to start conversations with ease.

For example, I was interested in learning how to speak better in public so I decided to join Toastmasters, a club dedicated to the learning and practice of good public speaking. I got to meet lots of interesting people who were very different from me (in terms of age, occupation, race, nationality), but we all had a common interest in public speaking, and so we got along well.

If you are already in a club or student group, you can become more active in it. That means volunteering to take on positions of responsibility or the organizing of events. It is a strange but beautiful paradox that the more you give, the more you get back in return. My eyes were opened to this when I was in the Students' Council at junior college. The people who were active and who dedicated their time and energy to our activities were the ones who gained the most from the experience.

Go to social events like dinners, parties or reunions. You can catch up with old friends and meet new people. All sorts of things can happen. It's the people staying at home refusing to participate who don't meet anybody.

You may ask: "What if I have no interests? What if I am the most boring person on earth and there is absolutely nothing I enjoy doing other than lying on my bed and sulking?"

Then I have to ask: How badly do you want to change? If you do not think you will be able to take the trauma of getting out of bed, putting a smile on your face and doing stuff with people then stay exactly where you are. See you later.

If you are willing to change, accept that it will be an uncomfortable process. Pick an activity that seems the least obnoxious to you and force yourself to go.

In my experience the best way to cure your feelings of loneliness is to go out there and brighten someone else's world. Shift the focus from you to them.

What if I have no friends?

If you have no friends at the current point in time, I have to make some unkind assumptions about you. Either you are:
1)   Hopelessly obnoxious
or
2)   Hopelessly shy
or perhaps you've been
3)   Brought up by a pack of wolves in the wilderness

If you are "1) Hopelessly obnoxious" please stay home and fantasise about making friends. No, no, I take that back. Go and irritate the heck out of everyone. Maybe, just *maybe*, some good (and foolish) Samaritan will show you kindness and friendship, and you can learn about being human again.

If you are "2) Hopelessly shy", start going to events that force you to interact with people (band camp anyone?). Once you are there grit your teeth to control the nervous shaking, smile and politely introduce yourself:

Fred: Hayee, ayem phreid!

Lisa: What?

Fred: Ayie shayed, ayem phreid!

Lisa: Maybe you should open your mouth when you speak?

Fred: Oh I'm sorry. I was just following the advice of this guy who said I should grit my teeth, smile and introduce myself.

Lisa: He must be an idiot. What was your name again?

If you are "3) Brought up by a pack of wolves in the wilderness", you can find lots of friends at the zoo. Good luck!

Saying hello can change your life

Nowadays, it's pretty easy to use instant messaging or social networking sites such as Friendster to meet all sorts of colourful characters. It's a convenient and non-threatening way to get to know people you would never meet in real life. But the typewritten word is a poor gauge of a person's mood and character. It's easy to invent a false personality to deceive someone else. Even if two people are genuinely trying to connect, lots of miscommunication can still take place. But it can be fun and interesting trading witty quips with a total stranger, so go ahead and try it if you're so inclined. Just remember to be careful and be realistic.

If you want to make friends you must take the initiative to thrash around the social jungles. You cannot be passive and hope someday opportunities to meet new and interesting people will flood your life. Often the hardest thing is to go up to someone, smile and say hello. But that simple thing could make an enormous difference to your life.

FRIENDSHIP FUNDAMENTALS

Some people use it promiscuously. Most of us use it for the people we come into pleasant contact with. "It" is the word "friend". There are two criteria a person must meet to earn the "friend" label:
1) There is mutual recognition and shared experience
2) The shared experience is rewarding

There is a continuum on which people you know and like can be placed on, and we shall look at these in increasing levels of intimacy:

+ **Acquaintances.** These are your typical "Hi! Bye!" type of friends. You probably know hundreds of such friends. These relationships are superficial, but the exchange of pleasantries and small talk can brighten your day.

+ **Circumstantial Friends.** All friendship is circumstantial (fate orchestrates the initial meeting between two people). The distinction is this: Are you simply friends because you share a similar set of circumstances? A majority of the friends you have made and will make are this sort. Most of your classmates, friends you meet through student groups and people you meet at camps and seminars are in this category. For the duration of the circumstance that has brought and kept you together, intimacy is created through shared conversations, activities and experiences. But these friendships often fade into obscurity once the common context changes – you graduate or change class, quit your student group or the camp ends. You discover that other than circumstance you shared very little in common with these people. Many people get cynical about friendships as a whole when they observe that their circumstantial friendships are unable to endure change.

+ **Your Outer Circle of Friends.** Not a cult, but the group of friends you have formed a deep and lasting bond with and whom you can depend on. You may not keep in regular contact with them, but once contact has been re-established, the friendship can be quickly brought back to its previous level of intimacy.

However, the friendship will stagnate without active nurturing. You can probably count these friends on your fingers and toes, and in a way, these friends are like them – not the arms and legs your closest friends are, but still important parts of your social anatomy.

✦ **Inner Circle/Best Friends.** The Holy Grail of friendship, you trust these friends so completely you can be your true self with them. No fart is too smelly, no burp too disgusting, no confession too horrifying to them. They accept you as you are. Trust is a sacred aspect of your closest friendships. You trust your friend to act in your best interests. There is regular contact and rejuvenation of these friendships. Most of us are lucky to have one or two of these.

I write this with a tinge of regret and a dollop of gratefulness. Regret because of the many friends by circumstance I have lost contact with that could have been brought into my Outer Circle or even Inner Circle of friends – there have been many missed opportunities to deepen a friendship. And I feel grateful for the few Inner Circle friends I have held on to. They have taught me much. They have looked past my flaws and seen my potential instead. They have shown me what it means to be a friend, to have an unconditional hand of friendship to hold.

How do you tell a true friend from the riffraff? A true friend will:

✦ Help you if it is within his power to do so, even at his own expense, but will refuse to help when doing so is not in your long-term interest
✦ Not judge you, but will honestly criticise your unacceptable behaviour
✦ See the potential in you and nurture it
✦ Separate the stupid things you do once in a while from the person you are

To find a true friend, be one. If you find a true friend, cherish him or her for a lifetime.

Winning them over

To be liked, be sincerely interested. You won't go far by manipulating someone to like you. Most people are perceptive enough to pick up on phoniness, and they'll resent you for it. You have to truly care about the other person. Find the wisdom within telling you life is less about you and what you can get from it, and more about others and what you can do for them.

That being said, the technical aspects of making friends might be of value to you if they're impeding the progress of your social life. Here are the basics of making friends:

◆ **Converse.** Good conversation is a game of give-and-take. You ask questions and acknowledge his or her expressed interests or values. You then share parts of your life, with the understanding he or she will reciprocate and acknowledge your views. Of course, when you're actually talking you aren't conscious of this dynamic, as the words flow and you lose track of time. If you are artificial or self-conscious in your conversation it will show. Let what you say be a reflection of who you are.

◆ **Smile.** A good way to release any tension present in the conversation is to smile. A smile is a universal expression of warmth, goodwill and friendship.

◆ **Eye contact.** Make eye contact to communicate your interest and sincerity. It's been said that your eyes are the windows to your soul, and people who avoid making eye contact run the risk of being misinterpreted as having something to hide.

The first impression you make on a person goes a long way to colour the perception that person will have of you, so make it a good one. It's much easier than trying to reverse a negative first impression. As far as possible, be authentic and rewarding to other people – make them feel better about themselves after talking to you.

The good that friends can do

Perhaps you are a hermit who has lived your entire life in an isolated hut. There, you have the call of the birds, the soothing scent of the forest and the bustle of the chimpanzees. You may ask: "Why have friends at all?" That is a valid question. Why have friends? What benefits does friendship bring?

Friends provide companionship. You spend time doing things together instead of curling up on your bed alone. Their company enlivens your life, and their ideas and experiences can challenge your thinking. Stories and news of themselves or others bring novelty and stimulation into your life. We all have a desire for entertainment and recreation, and socializing with friends via a shared activity like a game of squash or over a cup of coffee is a good way to meet those wants.

Friends are also a source of emotional support. Our self-esteem and egos need caring for. There are times when you need a friend for affirmation or a listening ear. Close friends empathise when we are unhappy by listening to our troubles and making us feel loved. Research has shown that people with strong friendships lead longer, happier lives.

Friends help each other. They can do this in a tangible way – for example, by lending you money. Or it can be in an intangible way, by providing you with an extra brain to help you clarify, understand and solve your problems.

Finally, friends are a great way to learn more about yourself and the world around you. There are parts of your personality and character which you cannot see – your blind spots. You need friends to help you see yourself from a different, detached perspective. You will be amazed at how much you do not know about yourself. From the animal rights of ants to the thrill of go-kart racing, friends can also show you a side of the world you never knew existed.

BUILDING LASTING FRIENDSHIPS

The friends you choose will have a big impact on your life, so don't let chance and boredom dictate whom you spend time with. Your friends influence the kind of person you become – the way you talk, your opinions and your attitude towards life. Others will take the kind of people you hang out with as a reflection of who you are ("birds of a feather flock together").

You *can* choose whom you spend your time with. Consciously choose to be with people who support, uplift and inspire you, who make you laugh and who force you to take yourself less seriously. Choose to be with people you admire and respect – the go-getters, self-starters and live-wires. People who are happy, positive, kind and generous. People who stimulate you to think deeper and who open your eyes to new ways of looking at things. People you can learn from, whom you want to emulate.

Similarly, choose to limit the influence of people who patronise or depress you. They will stifle and drag you down to their level of thinking. You only have a limited amount of time and energy, and as much as you wish you could, cannot possibly become best buddies with everyone.

Make a list of all the people you know. Think about how you spend your time with them. Are you spending the most time with people you care about and respect? Or are you hanging out with a group of friends you know are a bad influence on you? Sometimes it's fun to hang out with the "bad" crowd and let yourself loose. It's fine as long as you don't do anything you'd regret afterwards.

Your choice of friends will colour the kind of person you become. Choose wisely.

Friends forever

Building a friendship is as simple as this: To have a friend, be a friend. Being a friend is about extending your self to another person, about sharing your thoughts, feelings, activities, material things and time with him or her. It involves regular contact with that person, and it requires both parties to be committed and active in developing the friendship. Sometimes you will take the initiative to invite the person out for a movie, and sometimes she will call you for a cup of coffee. If your friendship is not growing it is stagnating, or worse, wilting.

Friends listen to each other. Many of us think having a conversation with someone means we have to be interesting, to think of all sorts of witty replies to throw in when the other person has finished talking. If you have ever spoken with someone who has a canned reply to everything you say, you walk away feeling a sense of unease because everything this person says is so superficial. Friends listen for your true feelings and motivations. They are not quick to judge, but accept you for who you are. People often do not say what they mean, and friends try their best to de-code the signals. This is not easy, but friends try anyway.

Friends spend time together. This does not mean you have to be physically together. There can be a meeting of minds and souls when you write letters or emails to each other.

Friends have fun, and are not afraid to be creative, to try new things and explore new ideas. With my friends, I have done things I would never have done on my own, such as dancing on an arcade machine!

Friends think about each other. This is not just about remembering birthdays, but also about giving a friend a call when you have not spoken in a while, sending her a card or a present out of the blue, and reminiscing about all the wacky things you have done together. It's the little things that count.

Friends are themselves with each other. This takes time, but with people you trust you will crawl out of your shell. You feel vulnerable and scared when you are yourself and have no masks on, but in the presence of a friend who will not take advantage of your vulnerability and who accepts you as you are, the feeling of being your true self is liberating.

Time is needed to forge deep and lasting friendships; take the initiative and put in effort to craft a true masterpiece.

Seven Sure-fire Ways To Sever Your Friendships

Now that we've talked about how to make friends, what about how *not* to do it?

1) By complaining all the time
Are you a whiner? Are the phrases "I'm bored" and "Life sucks" constantly on the tip of your tongue? This is the disease of negativity, and if you have it others will avoid you like a leper.

2) By shamelessly sponging off them
Not just in a material (money, stuff) way, but also in terms of effort. Do you pay for your fair share? Do your part in group activities? Are you ever the one to organise outings and get-togethers?

3) By putting on a façade
It is funny how we put on masks thinking we can get away with it while at the same time being acutely aware of the masks others are putting on. Do you try to conceal your ugly side fearing your friends will abandon you? Do you want your friends to like you for who you are or who you pretend to be?

4) By constantly making excuses for your inexcusable behaviour
I used to have a problem with punctuality. I found it difficult to be on time for anything – meeting up with friends, going to school – especially if there were no harsh penalties for being late. With some friends who had similar habits, it degenerated into a ludicrous situation where we both thought "he's gonna be late so I might as well go later." As you can imagine, we were lucky to meet before the cows came home from the moon and the pigs made it to Mars. This bad behaviour constituted a withdrawal from the bank account of friendship we had built up. When all you do is make excuses instead of tackling the root of the problem, your friends will find you inconsiderate.

5) By hurtfully criticizing them and being overly negative
Do you know people who are sceptical and critical about everything you say and do? They are the first to find fault with and tear apart any ideas you have. They bad-mouth you in front of others, and they belittle your achievements. If so, you have probably stayed far, far away.

6)   By ignoring them when you have better things to do

Do you know people who call you out when they're bored, but are icy towards you at other times? A disregard for others when you are having a good time will drive them away when they realise they are only your backup option.

7)   By betraying their trust

Can your friends trust you with their secrets? Or do they believe you will immediately broadcast it to the whole world? Can they trust you to act in their best interests? Can they trust you to tell the truth? The worst scenario is when your friends already know the truth and they see you blatantly lying to them. Say goodbye to integrity, trust and…friendship.

All of us act in one or more of these seven ways once in a while. When it happens admit your mistakes, apologise sincerely and make the effort to change.

OVERCOMING SHYNESS

We all feel it from time to time – that feeling of extreme self-consciousness, of being under a magnifying glass where our every word and action is scrutinised. We withdraw, not daring to risk embarrassment and rejection.

Shyness is social anxiety, the opposite of social confidence. If you feel nervous and uncomfortable in some social situations, such as talking to someone of the opposite sex or a stranger, your shyness is situational. Most of us suffer from situational shyness, and it is a normal thing. Others might feel shy in virtually all social situations; their shyness is chronic.

Shyness is a matter of degree. You are not either "shy" or "not shy", but somewhere between being shy in very few situations or shy in most situations. Where you lie on that scale can be identified by how often you experience the following:

- ✦ Blushing
- ✦ Feeling tongue-tied
- ✦ Not making eye contact
- ✦ Not knowing what to say
- ✦ Being excessively self-critical

If you often feel these things in the presence of others, your shyness is chronic and habitual.

Breaking the shyness habit

A first step towards breaking this habit is to stop thinking of yourself as a shy person, but instead as someone who behaves in a shy way in certain social situations. It is more constructive to think of shyness as a habit rather than an unchangeable personality trait. Think of it as unchangeable, and it will become a self-fulfilling prophecy.

Breaking the shyness habit requires desensitization. You need to expose yourself to the very situations you are afraid of. Perhaps not directly and all at once, but in small, manageable steps. It takes time to unlearn this habit so don't expect overnight miracles. Gradually push yourself out of your comfort zone. Start by making use of the least threatening avenues of communication like email or chatting online. Use the telephone as a confidence-building tool to lessen your anxiety of interacting with another human being.

Talk about yourself and your interests. You can't expect the other person to do all of the talking. You have to share some information about yourself as well.

If possible, join acting or public speaking classes. In these classes you will have the opportunity to shed your inhibitions in a less threatening environment. It can be lots of fun, and you'll also learn useful skills.

A person who is socially confident, who doesn't care so much about how others respond to him will, paradoxically, be more well-liked and found to be more interesting. Shy people, on the other hand, are often misunderstood to be cold, withdrawn and uninterested when they are really just afraid. Realise the cost of shyness to your life, and you will realise the effort involved in overcoming it is well worth taking.

The curse of craving popularity

Shy, lonely people often crave popularity. They think it's the answer to their misery ("I wouldn't feel so lousy about myself if only I was popular.") They see the popular people being on such friendly terms with everyone and they wonder why they weren't born with such luck. Being popular does have its benefits, but it isn't the antidote to loneliness and a poor self-image.

A popular person is well-known and well-liked by many members of a group. But being popular means you have to divide your social energy across a large number of people. You have to be careful of spreading yourself too thin, or risk watering down all of your relationships, especially the ones that should be deep and meaningful. Some popular people find themselves friends with everyone but close friends with no one.

Some popular people need to be liked by everyone they meet. But they simply can't please everyone no matter how hard they try, and so never get to enjoy the benefits their popularity brings, instead suffering the misery of knowing a few people dislike them. Craving popularity for popularity's sake will only leave you dissatisfied, and you are likely to neglect the friends who truly value you.

There's nothing wrong with wanting to be popular, but thinking that becoming popular is the way to fill the emptiness you feel inside will backfire – the more popular you are, the lonelier you feel.

Uniquely me

Instead of trying to be someone else to win the favour of others, be yourself and get along with people by:

1) Being approachable and friendly
Being approachable means being receptive to meeting and talking to people. Some people constantly have a frowned expression on their face which sends the message "Go away! Leave me alone!" to everyone who sees them. Relax and smile. Being friendly means you also take the initiative to talk to people, to make them feel liked and welcome.

2) Being considerate of others
Know when it is best to persist in your friendly efforts and when it is best to leave people alone and let them be. If you see someone in deep concentration reading a textbook it is best not to interrupt.

3) Making a conscious effort to listen to people
Truly listening to someone is a difficult thing to do. Pay attention the next time you talk to someone. When the other person speaks, are you consciously absorbing what the person has to say or are you trying to think of what to say next? From the person's words and body language, are you able to get a hint of the person's true meaning and feelings? People often do not say what they really mean or feel, and only by paying attention can you uncover their underlying messages.

4) Not trying to please everyone
It is more important to have a few good friends than a horde of acquaintances. Do not spend your life trying to please and humour everyone around you. Some people do this in an effort to be liked, often at the

expense of their own happiness. It is futile and will often have the opposite effect because we do not respect people who do not respect themselves.

5) Developing your talents

You earn the respect of your peers (and your parents) when you expend effort in the mastery of a skill (e.g. playing a musical instrument or sport) or in a meaningful activity (e.g. helping out in an old folks' home or working part-time to earn your pocket money). Be responsible for developing your talents to the fullest, and aim to excel in a particular area.

6) Being yourself

There is no need to be something different to different people. Perhaps you act or speak in an "in" way with a certain group or clique and change like a chameleon with another group. Genuine people have congruence between who they are and the way they act – they are the same with all people.

7) Accepting that not everyone will like you

I know a girl who's almost universally beloved – she is super friendly, sweet, genuine, sincere and never has a bad thing to say about anybody. I say *almost* universally beloved because there are a few people out there who dislike her for being so "saccharin sweet" and "goody-two-shoes". You cannot win all the time. Accept it.

Instead of seeking popularity, strive to be more rewarding in your relationships with others. Instead of being Mr./Ms. Popularity, let people know you as Mr./Ms. Really-Great-Friend-To-Have.

YOUR OWN BEST FRIEND

I once talked to a friend who was recounting the conversations she had with various people during the day. In each of those conversations, she spoke of the various witty comments she made and the flattering responses she received. After a while, it seemed to me her recall of her conversations was more to portray how smart and endearing she was than to share what she actually experienced during the day. I went away from that conversation with nagging doubts about the accuracy of her description, while getting little chance to know the real her.

We all have insecurities. We all have painful, unflattering moments. Some of us like to pretend those do not exist, that we do not have dark sides. Trust is needed before you dare to lower your defences and let your real self shine through. To bring your relationships to a deeper level you have to tell the truth about your feelings, thoughts and opinions, even if it reflects on you negatively, because that is who you really are.

I'm still struggling to share more of my inner world with my closer friends. A friend once described me as a "closed person", because I am often hesitant to reveal my deeper thoughts and feelings about a situation or a person. Thus the people who know me better may ironically find me to be emotionally distant. I think I have improved since I was described as a "closed person", but still have a long way to go.

Learning to expose more of yourself to people (not literally – that's illegal!) is a process littered with pitfalls. You are likely to trip and fall along the way, but it's perfectly fine to make mistakes as long as you learn from them, get up and move on.

Know thyself

Friends are vital to your well being, but they're not everything. It is important to allocate time for your own personal growth as well. Spend time to improve yourself, develop your skills and enrich your mind.

You also need time for yourself to rest and reflect on all that is happening in your life. Sometimes we're too immersed in our day-to-day lives to notice and learn the lessons life is trying to teach us. Taking time off to think through things will give you the perspective you need. Your body, mind and soul have the opportunity to recharge while you are resting.

There was a period of time when I had an extremely active social life. I was out almost every night with different friends to have dinner, watch movies or just bum around. I don't really remember much from that time, probably because so much was happening. After a few weeks this overactive social life began to take its toll. I was exhausted and broke. I was glad when I finally had a chance to stay home and lie on my couch. Okay, so I'm not the most sociable person in the world, but anyone would get tired after a while. The point? Even play can be tiring if you do too much of it. You need to rest as well. And here comes that magical word again – balance.

There are people who cannot stand being alone. They need to meet up with their friends or even people whose company they do not enjoy to escape being by themselves. They cannot stand their own company. But ultimately, you are alone in this world. No human being can ever think your thoughts or feel your feelings, or know what it is like to be you. Get to know yourself and enjoy your company first, and then you can build a sturdy connecting bridge to others.

Part 4
That Special
Someone

Brief Contents

THE TRUTH ABOUT JACK AND JILL

Love is perhaps the most ambiguous word of all. Unfortunately, we only have one word to describe the many faces of human attachment. Sociologist John Lee proposes six different types:

- ✦ **Passionate love (eros)** concentrates on physical attraction and the satisfaction of the senses. Those who are in its hold seek fast developing, intense relationships.
- ✦ **Friendship love (storge)** grows from a friendship based on shared interests and hobbies. It is a considerate and thoughtful kind of love.
- ✦ **Possessive love (mania)** is an insecure and dependant kind of attachment. Possessive lovers are often anxious and fearful of rejection, and become jealous easily.
- ✦ **Selfless love (agape)** is a sacrificial, unconditional type of love. Selfless lovers give without expecting a return.
- ✦ **Practical love (pragma)** is level-headed, realistic and calculating. Practical lovers seek to find partners who come from a suitable background, who can satisfy the tangible and intangible benefits they seek.
- ✦ **Game-playing love (ludus)** is a playful and fun type of love, with little real commitment involved. Game-playing lovers are flirtatious, and enjoy keeping their partners guessing.

Even though love can be classified into these six categories, it does not mean relationships can be put neatly into any one box. Love is dynamic – it changes over time. Some people experience passionate love for one another, but with the passage of time and deeper interaction, a more relaxed friendship love begins to emerge.

Everyone attaches a different meaning to the idea of love. What does love mean to you? The wisest young person I know – my friend Ann – shared with me her views on what love means to her:

Love to me is the sharing of my entire being – mind, body, heart and soul – with another human being in the way that I never can do with anybody else, which is easier said than done. It's finding the missing part of my life which I never realised was missing. It's finding something deeper, greater than my most fulfilling friendship, finding the soul mate.

Love isn't about "settling" for something less, it lets you grow wings to fly higher than you ever thought you could before. Love empowers you. And true love humbles you, because it makes you realise that you're no longer the most important person in the world to yourself.

Love is about changing from the "I" mentality to the "We", from asking "What will make me happy?" to "What will make us both happy?". You have come to the state where you cannot be happy unless your other half is happy too. It's about giving, and loving it. It's about sharing your life, not just parts of your life you designate to be "shared", but wishing to share every part of your life with someone. Love is about transparency.

And on top of that, I really believe and agree in the biblical definition and discussion of love in 1 Corinthians 13:4-8: "Love is patient, love is kind. It does not envy, it does not boast, it is not proud. It is not rude, it is not self-seeking, it is not easily angered, it keeps no record of wrongs. Love does not delight in evil but rejoices with the truth. It always protects, always trusts, always hopes, always perseveres. Love never fails."

I also find truth in M. Scott Peck's (author of *The Road Less Travelled*) definition of love: "The will to extend one's self for the purpose of nurturing one's own or another's spiritual growth."

Fast food love

Some people hurry into relationships to experience the intense rush of feelings. The media and peer pressure exert a strong influence – your expectations are formed by watching movies, reading romance novels, listening to love songs and seeing your peers pair off. You imagine how wonderful it is to be in love – that perfect, floating feeling. It is easy to fall in love with love (as opposed to a person), to seek the feeling as an end in itself.

Meanwhile your hormones are wreaking havoc on your body and mind and you begin to fixate on attractive members of the opposite sex. If there is mutual attraction, you jump headfirst into a relationship, thrilled by the opportunity to be in *lurve*.

Unfortunately, these relationships are often shallow and short-lived. Though you might feel you love the other person with all your heart and soul, you are often not in love with your partner, but with an idealised version of him or her, an image of perfection. You are blind to his or her faults.

Once the intense feelings of romance wears off, disappointment and disillusionment quickly set in. You notice things that irritate you, such as the way he "acts cool" or the way she complains about everything. You quarrel, ignore each other, then realise you do not really like each other in the first place. A break-up occurs, or the unhappy relationship is dragged out, resulting in even more hurt and frustration. One party ignores the other, and the other feels rejected and abandoned.

"Fast food love" is about entering a relationship before you are ready and mature enough to do so. Often the quicker it begins the quicker it ends. A happy ending is rare, as disenchantment sets in once the excitement wears off. And when things start to go wrong they can throw you into bouts of anxiety and depression. You cannot fill your feelings of loneliness by chasing the thrill of romance, diving headlong from one relationship into another.

Preparing yourself for love

The particular danger of adolescent love is that you fall in love at a time when it may affect your education or career-path decisions. In other words, the rest of your life. Entering into a sexual relationship may also lead to pregnancy, which casts an enormous burden onto young people who have not yet learnt to handle life. Such rash choices have lifelong repercussions.

As romance is such an overwhelming emotion, some lose interest in spending time with their studies, friends, hobbies or family. By the time they crash down from the peak of passion, much time has been lost and irreversible damage done.

We have a need to identify with our peers and obtain their approval – having no boyfriend or girlfriend might make you feel unattractive and unwanted, not just to the opposite sex, but to your same sex friends as well. I know it is tough to withstand peer pressure to get a boyfriend or a girlfriend, but don't jump into a relationship before you are ready.

Preparing yourself for love involves developing your own self and personality. You have to be comfortable with being you, independent of the approval of others. Of course, we can't help being affected by others' opinion of us, but we learn to take it as it is, and not let them dictate how we see ourselves or the things we do. Learning to be self-sufficient and independent will enable you to bring more to a future relationship – you have your own opinions, hobbies, interests, abilities and talents.

While you're still at an exploratory stage, you should expand your social circle by making more friends of both sexes. This allows you to be comfortable interacting with others, not to mention that stable relationships often develop from a solid base of friendship.

My friend Ann also shared her views on how one should prepare oneself for a relationship, and I know she is a living example of her beliefs:

> I think that before a person is ready for a romantic relationship, he or she has to be mature and must first reach a certain level of self-understanding and enlightenment about himself (or herself). What do I mean? When we look at most teen relationships, most of them don't last. And it's not just the overused explanation of "they're too young and immature", because maturity isn't dependent on age after all, and there are very mature teenagers around.

I think the problem is that a lot of people enter relationships before they really know what they want – in their lives and in their relationships. Contrary to popular practice or belief, the "trial and error" way of finding "the one" isn't the best or wisest way. That trail has left many broken hearts that can never be the same again. Some people have been trying for so long and still have not "wizened" up to the HOW. And while some people might get lucky and stumble upon "the one", that may still not predict a happy and stable relationship.

There aren't many people who think that love needs preparation, but it does indeed. Because when you really know what you're seeking in life and in a mate (and it's not as simple as it seems), there really aren't that many people who can fit. You know how when I was 8 the criteria for my guy was 'tall, dark, handsome, prince preferably'? And that was different when I was 14, 16, 18, 20 ... I have gradually refined what I really am seeking, and what's really important to me, and by the time I knew, I'd already whittled it down so that when I found the guy, I knew that he's the only one.

It's not really just becoming more selective, but getting wiser to your own needs, your dreams and what's really important to you, and that also helps in realizing what kind of things are important to you in a relationship, what kind of person will fit you, and how you want to love.

UNDERSTANDING ATTRACTION

Why do you find someone attractive and someone else repulsive? There are reliable factors to explain your attraction to some people and not others:

✦ **Appearance.** A person's physical appearance is the first thing that strikes you about him or her. What is considered beautiful varies across cultures, and societal norms change over time (e.g. being plump has been a hallmark of attractive women in many cultures in the past). It is not just the physical features but also their presentation that influence your impression. The person's dress sense (fashionable or square?), tone of voice (warm or reserved?), level of assertiveness (assured or nervous?) and body language (open and smiling or closed and frowning?) are all important parts of the package.

✦ **Similarity.** Over time, as you get to know this person better, the degree of similarity between the two of you will strongly influence the level of attraction that occurs. This similarity includes worldviews ("Man is basically good"), values ("Family is the most important thing in life"), tastes ("Classical music is superior to trashy pop") and beliefs ("The death sentence is inhumane").

✦ **Expectations.** We are drawn to people who match our preconceived "image" of our ideal partner. This "image" is usually a set of physical and personal qualities drawn and put together from the role models in our lives – parents, people we admire and cultural icons like pop stars. Sociologists offer an alternative theory of negative attraction. Instead of looking for qualities we find attractive, we screen out characteristics we dislike. If you are a guy who dislikes thin, pretty girls with long hair, anyone possessing these attributes "fails" and is deemed unattractive in your eyes.

Mars vs. Venus

There are gender-based differences in the personal qualities that guys and

68

girls find attractive in each other. Surveys have shown that the qualities girls look for in guys include:

✦ Leadership qualities
✦ A sense of humour
✦ Athleticism
✦ Financial stability
✦ Intellect

So is it true that guys only go for looks? Guys do go for looks, but it is not the only criteria they have. The qualities that guys look for in girls include:

✦ Physical attractiveness
✦ Warmth and affection
✦ Dress sense
✦ Sensitivity to others' needs
✦ Artistic creativity

Can you become more attractive?

In a bid to increase their level of physical attractiveness, many people use beauty products to enhance their features and hide their flaws. Girls use concealers and powders to cover blemishes, lipsticks to emphasise the curves and colour of their lips, and eye shadow to highlight and draw emphasis to their eyes. Guys use hair gel to hold up messy and shapeless hair, and shave or grow their facial hair to enhance a clean look or to project a rugged masculinity.

Both sexes rely on applied scents (perfume for girls and cologne or aftershave for guys) to enhance their attractiveness. Attraction occurs not just on a visual level, but also on an olfactory one.

Both environmental (external circumstances) and genetic factors contribute to your attractiveness. Your physical features (e.g. bone structure, body type) are heavily influenced by your genes. It has been found that genes are also responsible for certain personality traits, but these are expressed as tendencies and not absolutes. In other words, you cannot blame your genes for the choices you make. They influence your behaviour but do not control you.

If your genes are such an important factor in determining your level of attractiveness, does that mean you have no hope of becoming more attractive if you bear a closer resemblance to Frankenstein than Tom Cruise? The answer is no.

Your genes determine the boundaries you have to work within, but it is up to you to decide how far to push them. You can exercise and watch your diet, or learn to be more friendly and considerate. You can develop your athletic, intellectual and artistic potential. You can pay greater attention to the way you dress and the image you project to other people. You can even develop a sense of humour by looking at the lighter side of life.

Almost anyone can become more attractive if they are willing to invest the effort to honestly appraise themselves and work on their weak areas. If life gives you a lemon, compose a citrus-scented perfume.

DATING 101

Whether you are a guy or girl thinking of making a move on your target, the question remains: How do you get that Big First Date?

You could start by making cameo appearances – turning up by "coincidence" at places where your target hangs out. You could even attempt to make a deep and lasting impression by doing daring stunts such as riding a bicycle on one wheel with no hands, and then losing your balance and tumbling into a drain. Appearing in bandages and a cast later will also be an effective play on stirring up pity. But don't overdo it and become a stalker; the only date you'll have then is one with the police.

A side note: Despite the huge advances made by the feminist movement since the time of Emmeline Pankhurst, it remains a sad fact today that guys generally have to take the initiative in bridging the gulf between the sexes. But it is time for daring, courageous gals to shrug off labels such as "desperate" and "cheap" to wrest the conch of control from the callous cads of chauvinism. No longer should girls have to wait by their cell phones (or computers) for guys to call (or message) them. Go for it, girls! Boldly approach the boys you like. GIRL POWER!

The approach

Some "champions" with nerves of steel elect to take the Gung-Ho Approach, which involves walking straight up to their target and asking in-your-face for his or her number, or even for a date.

They believe in the Law of Large Numbers: for every ninety-nine people who will simply ignore them, splash some juice onto their jeans or slap them, there will be one who, completely drunk after taking a large number of tequila shots, accidentally divulges his or her number.

If this is your style, go for it. I'd recommend asking for an email address or instant messaging nickname though, as it puts less pressure on your target. But most feel this approach is too risky. We are mice, not men. We are mushrooms, not oaks. We are guppies, not sharks. You get the point.

The alternative is the Attrition Approach. This involves repeated exposure to create familiarization. You regularly approach your target to chat about homework or gossip. What you want to do is whittle away the barriers of resistance in his or her mind. You are looking for an inroad.

Of paramount importance is the ability to properly read the signals. If after a hundred such approaches the conversation with your target remains as such:

You: Hi there!

Target: Go away.

You: Isn't it a beautiful day?

Target: Get lost.

You: You wanna go see a movie?

Target: I'm calling the police.

... then you should learn to let go and move on, or risk being body slammed by her muscle-bulging, rugby-playing brother with a crooked nose.

But if the signals are ambiguous, you still have a chance. Your best bet is to wait it out, to control your hormonal urges and lay down the firm foundations of a solid friendship. Clarify the signals – does she think of you only as a friend, does he think of you as a little sister?

Sometimes you find you lack the confidence to take action. I have always been afraid of imposing on somebody else and of being disliked, which prevented me from exploring the opportunities that have come my way, not just for relationships but also for friendships.

Courage, it has been said, is not the lack of fear but action in the face of fear. If you think you've got a chance, trust your gut and go ask for a date. The worst that can happen is you'll get rejected. You'll get over it. I promise.

The date

So you've got that Big First Date, now what? You want to create the ideal impression, to get it right. First decide what to do. Dating activities can generally be split into three categories:

- ✦ **Typical.** Run-of-the-mill activities include watching movies, drinking coffee or having lunch/dinner. These are considered "safe" activities, and give you a chance to interact with your date in a non-threatening situation. However, these activities may be considered by some as a sign of your lack of creativity.
- ✦ **Active.** Move that body! Possible dates to get the heart pumping and the adrenaline flowing include racket sports (tennis, badminton, squash) and wheel sports (cycling, blading, go-kart racing).
- ✦ **Wacky.** Want to be different from everyone else? How about extreme water sports like wakeboarding? It's sure to be an experience you'll remember, *if* you make it back alive. The library is another alternative, and scholastically-inclined lovebirds can cosy up behind isolated shelves of books, looking up naughty subjects in the encyclopaedia.

Whatever type of dating activity you choose, make sure it allows you to have a shared positive experience, and that it encourages conversation. You do want to get to know the other party better, don't you?

Here are some suggestions to making your date a successful one:

- ✦ **Focus on being interested, not interesting.** Don't try to charm your date by thinking of witty and intelligent things to say, and in the process fail to listen to what he or she is actually saying. Practice really listening – still your mind and concentrate solely on the ideas your date is communicating to you.
- ✦ **Be gracious and considerate.** Turning up on time for the date is the obvious one. While on the date itself, refrain from bad-mouthing others you know, spewing vulgarities or creating any sort of scene. Be the perfect gentleman or lady.
- ✦ **Take your time to get to know the other person.** There is no point trying to hurry the date. Often, trying to rush a relationship will only lead to its earlier demise.

✦   **Be yourself.** We put on a fake front all the time – acting in a "cool" way to impress her, or purring demurely to attract him. We fear our real selves too boring or unattractive to actually catch anyone's fancy. Perhaps that's true. Better to find out sooner than later.

Above all, enjoy yourself! It is just a date after all.

Should I get attached?

Dating is a way for people to sieve out potential long-term partners (amongst other motives, but I will focus on this one). It is a process of discovery.

For young people who are insecure about their identities or are learning to handle the demands of life and school, getting involved in a serious relationship could throw their lives off-balance. Intense romantic feelings are transient, and what you thought was eternal yesterday could be a painful memory tomorrow.

It is healthier to take this dizzying stage of life as a "sampling stage", where you go on casual dates (perhaps in groups) to learn more about and to become comfortable interacting with members of the opposite sex.

If you do find someone whom you are interested in and want to become "more than friends", make sure you are able to keep the relationship in perspective. There are other parts of your life like your academic work, extracurricular involvement, family life and friends you do not want to neglect.

Take these experiences as a chance for you to learn about relating to someone else, about managing your feelings and learning to handle the different parts of your life. Well handled, this period of your life can be a sweet one.

DEVELOPING MEANINGFUL RELATIONSHIPS

Is it foolish to search for wholeness in a relationship when you can only be two separate individuals? We are ultimately alone – no other human being can think our thoughts or experience our unique combination of joys and sorrows.

But two people can share moments of togetherness on a regular basis if they learn how to do it properly. Terence Gorski, author of *Getting Love Right*, says there are actually three individuals in a relationship – You, Me and Us. Gorski observes that many people mistakenly believe love is a mysterious phenomenon beyond their control. On the contrary, healthy love is not an accident but a decision – a relationship is an agreement to meet each other's needs.

If only finding "the one" was as easy as this:

- ✦ You meet someone and there is mutual attraction
- ✦ You go out on a date and enjoy each other's company
- ✦ You go out on a few more dates and discover you have much in common
- ✦ You fall in love and decide to enter into a relationship
- ✦ The more time you spend with each other and the more you learn about each other, the more in love you are
- ✦ You decide to get married and live happily ever after

But the reality is that many, many things can go wrong at each stage of a relationship. It is tough enough to find someone who is closely tuned to your wavelength in terms of your values, habits and likes. Even if you do find someone like that, you may still find it difficult to get along with each other!

Continually learn about yourself and your patterns of behaviour, whether or not you are in a relationship. What do you want? What are you like? If you find you keep relating to people in a destructive or hurtful way, then that awareness is a key to unlocking this bad habit. If you wonder why your relationships always fail when you keep getting attached to the "wrong" type of person, you need to re-examine what you are really looking for.

Also, be clear about your goals for the relationship – are you looking for a short-term relationship or a long-term one? Does the other party know about it?

It's easy to jump into a romantic relationship with someone you do not know well. The passion of the moment often blinds you to your incompatibility. But these feelings fade fast, and all that's left may be the emptiness you began with and the realization of how shallow relationships can be. The best way to not get stuck in a disastrous relationship is to avoid entering one in the first place.

What are meaningful relationships like?

We need trusted friends and family to listen to us pour out our worries and dilemmas, or gabber inanely about nothing. We need them to encourage us when we are under pressure, support us when we are weak, and validate us as loveable human beings. A healthy romantic relationship is essentially the same thing, with the added dimension of attraction.

Wholesome, enduring relationships are characterised by a number of qualities:

✦ Honest, two-way communication
✦ A willingness to give and take
✦ A commitment to make the relationship work
✦ An ability to laugh together
✦ Patience
✦ Thoughtfulness
✦ Mutual respect

Relationships need to be regularly nourished. My friend Belle shared with me the steps she thought were necessary to develop a meaningful relationship:

Communication is fundamental to a relationship because people are unable to fully understand one another through their own limited perceptions. A meaningful relationship encompasses putting in our best effort to understand the other person, steer the relationship in a direction you want it to head in, and knowing where you stand in relation to each other. Often you may disagree with each other on all sorts of matters, but with good communication these disputes may be handled and resolved properly. Letting each other know your expectations of the relationship – for example, that you expect him or her to be there in your time of need, to ask and to show concern when you are feeling glum and so on – will prevent the scar of disappointment. Without communication, misunderstandings can easily occur.

Sharing is basically what relationships are about. This includes even the minutest details in life, like little niggling complaints to major life problems and difficulties. Opportunities for relationships to grow are present in both the good times and the bad times. Building a life together needs a commitment from two willing parties to work on the relationship. One of the greatest challenges in a relationship is not developing it but maintaining it.

Compromise is vital to every relationship. There can never be a satisfying relationship when the feelings and contribution towards the relationship of either party are unbalanced. A healthy amount of give-and-take is achieved by placing yourself in the other person's shoes, and by placing his or her feelings on par with your own.

Patience is the key to riding the ups and downs of any relationship, and to survive periods when either party is being unreasonable. Tolerance of the other person's bad habits, irritating idiosyncrasies and occasional obnoxious behaviour is necessary for the relationship to make it over the long haul. You also need a certain sense of stubbornness to hold on to the relationship as long as there is a glimmer of a chance that it will last – you can't just throw in the towel whenever you meet with a difficulty. Of course, if you believe there is no way the relationship can last, then you should end it.

Consistency in terms of your love and attention will provide a solid base on which to build the relationship. Blowing hot and cold can make the other party very insecure and damage the relationship. Time and trials experienced together will test your relationship and bring out aspects of the other person you may not have known existed.

Common relationship pitfalls

The following pitfalls will damage your relationships, so take corrective action if you spot them:

- ✦ Having unrealistic expectations of yourself, the other person or the relationship
- ✦ Coming too close too soon, physically or psychologically
- ✦ Being overly negative
- ✦ Trying to be a saviour
- ✦ Trying to change the other person
- ✦ Needing to always be right
- ✦ Stockpiling strong feelings – anger, pain, sadness, neediness – and then pouring them all out at once
- ✦ Expecting the other person to be a mind reader
- ✦ Crowding and smothering the other person, expecting him or her to meet all your needs and spend all his or her time with you

Perhaps you never imagined that relationships could be such hard work! But developing healthy ones certainly is, and in the process you not only have to work on building a bridge between two people, but also on sorting out who you are and what you want.

SURVIVING REJECTION, THRIVING AS A SINGLE

Your stomach feels on the verge of collapse, and your greatest impulse is to throw a blanket over yourself and mope. Welcome to the world of rejection. When the initial stage of denial ("this is not happening") is over, it is time to proceed through the lengthy process of grieving, picking up the pieces and moving on. Rejection is one of the most traumatic events that can occur in a young person's life. It can make you feel unwanted and inadequate.

If you have been rejected, remember:

✦ **Don't take it personally.** We often take another person's refusal to enter into a romantic relationship or discontinuation of one with us as a rejection of our entire self. We feel worthless, like a failure in life or God's big mistake. It is hard to imagine when you are in the throes of misery, but perhaps the reason is something other than you. Perhaps it was just not meant to be.

✦ **"This too shall pass."** Rejection is temporary. You will not be depressed and down in the pits of agony forever.

✦ **Keep your perspective.** Yes, rejection is painful. It can be devastating. But do not lose sight of the other important things in life – your friends, your family and your education.

✦ **Distract yourself.** Spending time with your friends, pursuing your hobbies, or even plunging yourself into your studies (YEAH!) will help to distract you while you recover. This is the time to take the French language class you've always wanted to, to organise a class party or to polish your piano skills. Choose to focus your attention and efforts on new and fun things.

✦ **For a while, keep a distance.** If possible, stay away from your "rejecter" until your emotional scars have healed. This does not mean to ignore the person or be unkind, but just to minimise contact because it's hard not to feel lousy when you see him or her.

✦ **Rediscover your friends.** Learn to appreciate the joy your friends bring to your life. Organise a slumber party, a picnic at the beach or an all-night Mah-jong session.

It takes time and effort to crawl out of the pit of rejection, but it can be done and you will recover.

It's swell to be a swinging single

So you've struck out, flunked in your pursuit of your prey. You feel like a beggar, possessing nothing. Well, you're wrong. You should be giving yourself a vigorous pat on the back for you now have:

✦ **Freedom.** You may spend your time in any way that pleases you. You are not tied down by another person. You are a free man (or woman).

✦ **Money.** No more splurging on flowers that wilt, teddy bears that go dusty or on expensive dinners that do not fill your tummy. You can start saving all that money for your future, or spend it any way you see fit.

✦ **Time.** Whereas previously you were booked every weeknight (for late-night calls) and on the weekends (for dates) you now have lots of free time.

So now you've got your freedom, money and time. Great. But what are you going to do with it? Here are some suggestions:

✦ **Develop yourself.** There is tons of unexplored potential in you. Recall the times you said the words "I wish I could …" or "If only I knew how to …" Take a course in pottery or read the great classics. Expand the frontiers of your skills and knowledge.

✦ **Nurture ties.** Your friends and family have taken a backseat for too long. It's time to catch up on all you've missed.

✦ **Relish your solitude.** You may be alone, but you need not feel lonely. Think about the things you've done, and what it says about you. Tell yourself a joke, then laugh hysterically.

✦ **Build new bonds.** By contributing your time and effort to a worthy cause, or by taking part in activities you are interested in, you greatly increase your chances of meeting others of like mind. Having a common interest and sharing a common experience will help break the ice.

Being single is often made out to be some sort of curse, a condition to be avoided at all costs. Do not believe it for a moment. Some people choose to remain single their whole lives. Why do you think they are called *swinging* singles?

Part 5
Schoolhouse Rock!

Brief Contents

WHY DO I HAVE TO GO TO SCHOOL?

I learnt the true value of my education at fifteen when I took a holiday job at a prestigious luxury hotel. Let me describe my job in greater detail. Guests checked into the hotel, and in doing whatever they do in hotel rooms they made use of both towels and bed sheets. When they checked out, the maids (not I) would gather the soiled linen and cart it off to a large central chute located in the back area of every floor. A five-star hotel might look grand, spotless and gleaming marble to you, but the back area where the staff work is often a slum.

Let's say the maids are cleaning rooms on the fifteenth floor. They stuff a bundle of linen into the chute, and this bundle hurtles downwards, accelerating according to the laws of gravity. Upon reaching the basement level, this bundle would pop out of the chute opening with a large WHOOMP and hurtle across an enclosed, windowless holding area, smashing into the opposite wall before falling onto the floor.

There I was in this stuffy, humid, lint-filled room, avoiding deadly cannonballs of linen while separating the mountain of towels and bed sheets into two carts. These were not your ordinary bed sheets and towels but the wet, stained, sticky, I-really-do-not-want-to-know-how-these-were-used type. Once these carts were full I would push them out of this room, down a hallway and load them onto a truck. Sounds like a dream job, doesn't it?

This was a daily-rated, low paying job with no chance of advancement whatsoever. Everyday I would line up at a counter to collect thirty dollars in cash for my ten hours of work. I worked there for a month.

After that experience, I felt a great desire to return to school, give my desk a kiss and study like I never did before. I felt then that the purpose of my education was to do so well I could sit in an air-conditioned office staring at a computer all day long for the rest of my life.

If you've ever worked at a job serving fast food or carrying crates of stuff around, you know the feeling of being trapped in an unrewarding, dead end job. People working in these jobs are often just trying to survive, to make enough money to put some food on the table for their families.

They have neither the skills nor the education to get a better job and carve out a more comfortable existence for themselves.

Education is your key to socioeconomic mobility. Even if you come from a poor family, if you make the most of your education and pick up some useful skills and knowledge, you have the opportunity to work in a more rewarding career, both financially and in terms of your job satisfaction. There is a direct correlation between your level of education and how much money you will make in a job.

Everyday in school when you're facing the whiteboard or a textbook, don't think in terms of trying to pass an exam; think in terms of building a better life for yourself and your family in the future.

Why you should get the best education you possibly can

Do you know why you are going to school? Is it only because you are expected to? If you find you drag yourself to school every morning, and would rather count the number of cracks on the ceiling than pay attention to the lesson, you need to know the advantages of having an education:

- ✦ **You have more opportunities in life.** With more doors open, you have more choices in life. My freedom is important to me, and if I'm able to earn enough to not have to worry about my day-to-day survival, I can begin to explore the possibilities in life. Your education is also something you can always fall back on. As my mom says, "Your business can go bankrupt, your shares can fall to zero, but your education is something no one can take away from you."

- ✦ **It stretches your mind.** With education, you gain a greater understanding of the world around you – how things work, why things are the way they are. Both the breadth (in terms of the number of things you know) and the depth (in terms of how well you know these things) of your insight will expand.

- ✦ **For the love of learning and knowledge.** Learning, if based on your interests, is fun and could even be exhilarating.

✦ **As a step towards maximizing your potential.** Don't let your brain go to waste. Your ability is only limited by your imagination.

See the bigger picture. Going to school and "getting an education" is not about textbooks, worksheets, grades and exams. It is about changing the lens through which you see the world, fitting you with wings to aid you on your journey through it, and giving you the master key to the locked doors of opportunity.

BECOMING AN "IDEAL" STUDENT

Presenting the cast ...

Aaron Athlete: More interested in rugby than his studies, Aaron nonetheless attempts to do his homework and read a few pages of his textbook when he's not too tired after training sessions. He does average during the off-peak season, but usually gets a failing grade during the tournament period.

Susan Slacker: Susan has a father who is a physics professor and a mother who is a doctor. Susan is perpetually sleepy (or "soporific" as she likes to call it) in class, never pays attention during the lesson, and spends little if any time doing her homework. When she does do her work, it is sloppy and barely legible. And yet due to her brilliance, she often manages to top the class though her results are erratic.

Neo Nerd: Neo is diligent in his work, perhaps to an extreme. He listens intently in class, copies down every point the teacher makes, memorises whole paragraphs from textbooks, and does exactly as he is told. He has never, in his whole schooling life, ever turned in an assignment late. Not even in kindergarten. Unfortunately, his results do not correspond with the effort he puts into his studies, and Neo is growing increasingly discouraged. He is beginning to think that he just doesn't have the brains.

Chris Curious: The class pest, Chris bombards the teacher during every lesson with a barrage of annoying questions. He cannot stop asking "Why?". He is so curious he often reads encyclopaedias and higher level material because he is dissatisfied with the teacher's answers. Though from the questions he asks he doesn't seem to know anything, he sometimes does surprisingly well. He is just as often found at the bottom of the grade curve.

8:45 A.M., Physical Geography

"So the earth's crust is like the broken pieces of an egg shell floating on an ocean of magma..."

Aaron clenches a tennis ball in his left hand, alternately flexing and relaxing his forearm muscles. He does it to strengthen his grip. His mind wanders off to the rugby game he saw on television the previous night. He thinks about the tactics of each team, and imagines himself scoring the winning try. A dreamy grin spreads across his face.

Her eyes half open, twirling her pen back and forth in her hand, Susan is gradually losing her battle with the Sleep Monster. Her notes are nothing more than illegible scribbles and ugly doodles. Susan has little tolerance for boredom, and finds it difficult to concentrate for long periods on anything she finds dull.

Neo, sitting on the edge of his chair, is paying full attention and transcribing the lesson. Reading his notes is like reliving the lesson, as they are an exact replica of what the teacher says, word for word.

"But Miss Loh, how is it possible that something as heavy as the earth's crust can float? Why doesn't it sink right through to the earth's core?" Chris asks.

Miss Loh is halfway through her explanation about how the lower relative density of the crust compared to the magma beneath it allows the crust to float when Chris interrupts her: "Okay, but why use egg shells as an analogy? Why not use lily pads in a pond instead? The pads overlap each other like the plates of the crust do, and there are convection currents in the pond as well."

While Miss Loh feels like screaming "Then why don't you go write the darn textbook yourself, you smart aleck!" at Chris, she does see that his example has some merit, and maybe even a hint of cleverness. She grudgingly acknowledges that, but proceeds to explain how the egg shell analogy more closely approximates the spherical shape of the earth.

Susan's interest is slightly piqued by the questions, but she soon drifts off to sleep again. Aaron, still daydreaming, is thrusting the large Champion's trophy up into the air triumphantly as the crowd cheers him. Neo dutifully copies Chris's questions and their answers down onto his notes.

9:30 A.M., Recess

At the ring of the recess bell, the class gasps a sigh of relief. Aaron retrieves the dumbbells he keeps in a corner of the classroom and proceeds to do three sets of bicep curls with twenty reps each. Susan, suddenly feeling invigorated, flips open her copy of *The National Geographic* and reads with fascination about the possible deluge of low lying islands by rising sea levels, an effect blamed on global warming. Neo is going through the lengthy notes he has made, trying to make sense of what happened during the lesson. Chris sits in deep thought for a moment, then rushes off to the library to read up on plate tectonics.

1:30 P.M., End of lessons

The school bell rings – lessons have ended for the day. Aaron grabs his sports bag and rushes out of the classroom. He's got to get something to eat before his training starts at two. He decides to take a look at the chapter on plate tectonics in his textbook later that evening if he's not too tired.

Susan heads home to play a strategy war game on her computer she's been hooked onto for the past week, and if she's bored she might entertain herself by working on some logic puzzles. Neo, too, returns home to reread his notes and try to memorise as much of it as he can. Chris makes his way to the Computer Room to surf the net for even more information on plate tectonics.

Questions to think about

Here are some questions for you to ponder:

+ Who does the best in tests? Susan tops the class without having to put in any apparent effort at all – a slacker smarty-pants. Chris sometimes comes out tops when he manages to give a relevant answer.

+ Who puts in the most effort? Neo – he's officially the class nerd. But somehow his efforts don't seem to pay off.

+ Who achieves the most balance? Aaron comes closest to this, as he is the only one with substantial extracurricular involvement. But he's paying too little attention to his schoolwork, especially during the tournament season.

✦ Who has learnt the most? Though his questions irritate the heck out of everyone, Chris takes the initiative to find things out for himself and manages to see the bigger picture of any concept, and with greater depth, compared to his classmates.

Who is the ideal student?

None of them are. They don't seem to have any social life at all, and they definitely have no class spirit!

✦ Aaron is disciplined in sports but is unable to transfer that discipline to his studies and ends up neglecting them.

✦ Susan has great potential but is wasting it because she does not put in effort even though she still manages to top the class.

✦ Neo is consistent and diligent, both positive traits. But just toughing it out does not necessarily translate to higher grades. Neo is unable to discriminate between what is important and what is not. He swallows information wholesale without fully understanding it.

✦ Chris shows curiosity, creativity and initiative in his learning but is unable to focus his vast store of knowledge about a particular subject to answer a test question. He often strays out-of-point, and gets penalised for his irrelevancy.

Is there such a thing as an ideal student?

Yes and no. Yes, because your situation is ideal if you are learning at your peak rate (maximum learning with minimum effort) and are able to use that learning. No, because everyone has his own style and there is no standard set of criteria to determine what an "ideal student" should be like.

The bottom line is, the successful student must be able to: i) Understand what is being taught and ii) Be able to apply it with good results in tests and other situations.

The price of inconsistency

Do you consistently do your homework and review what you have learnt? Or do you thrive under the pressure of the impending exam, preferring to cram huge amounts of material into your brain in a short time period? I've always been the latter. I never reviewed my work until days before the exam. I spent my primary school years playing computer games for hours each day. In secondary school, I upgraded to playing Mah-jong, and though things were getting pretty stressful a week or so before a major exam I still managed to cram enough in to scrape through.

Then in junior college, I began to feel the heat. My first term started off great with initial enthusiasm for the new subjects and challenges. This enthusiasm quickly became complacency, which then deteriorated into apathy. A month before the Preliminary Exams, I took the final Common Test and screwed up. Badly. That test proved to be the wake-up call I needed to shake myself from my intellectual sloth.

I knew I could not afford to screw this exam up and the Advanced Levels that followed, because together they would determine the opportunities available to me – things like whether I would be able to enter University or whether I would spend the rest of my days separating wet towels from sticky bed sheets.

And thus seven days a week, from noon to about ten o'clock at night, I isolated myself in a corner of the library and hit the books. My hard work finally did pay off, but I could have avoided a lot of suffering if I had applied myself consistently. I could have saved myself from consuming the huge amount of mints and snacks that stressed-out people binge on. I could have made prank calls to my friends who were all busy studying. I could have watched more episodes of my favourite cartoon, *The Simpsons*. Best of all, I could have had peace of mind.

If you do not want to end up like me:

- ✦ **Be consistent.** Daily effort allows you to thoroughly explore and cover the material without stressing yourself out.
- ✦ **Ensure you fully understand each topic as you cover it.** If not, bug your friends and teachers or read any basic text you can find on the subject until you thoroughly understand it.
- ✦ **Review your material constantly.** Almost nobody is able to capture and remember information fully on their first reading. You need to review it constantly to sink it deep into your long-term

memory. Memory expert Tony Buzan suggests this time frame – review the material ten minutes, one day, one week, one month and six months after you have first learnt it.

✦ **Rest well.** Make sure you have adequate amounts of relaxation, play and exercise. When you have completed what you planned to cover, go ahead and give yourself a reward – catch a movie with a friend, go out for dinner or just bum around on your couch.

Being consistent – doing your homework, reading your notes and textbook regularly, reviewing the material you have learnt before – is not just a tip to help you do better in your exams. It is a process of developing the discipline to help you succeed in life. Any worthwhile achievement is accomplished by chipping away at tasks and obstacles bit by bit. If you want to be successful in life you need to be focused and persistent, and it's best to develop these traits while you're in school.

INTERACTING WITH ALIENS (I.E. TEACHERS)

The possible existence of extraterrestrial intelligence in the universe poses a problem: How do we human beings communicate with it upon contact? We can make no assumptions about its methods of communication, because we have no idea what form this intelligence might take in the first place.

And should we assume this intelligence to be hostile or benevolent? We might antagonise it if we assume the former, but risk annihilation if we assume the latter. Perhaps it is best if we take the middle road of pacification and caution simultaneously, while learning as much as we can about its methods of communication and message.

Approach your teachers the same way. Some general principles:

+ There are great variations in personality and teaching styles among teachers, so you have to adapt your strategy for each one.
+ No one knows the whole truth. Do not take the words that come from your teachers' mouths as the absolute truth. Teachers too make mistakes and don't know all the answers.
+ Teachers are working professionals who require respect from you, and if you fail to show it they can make your life miserable.

Handling the aliens

How should you handle your teachers?

+ **Do not antagonise or offend them.** First of all, attend class. Take note that in subjects like Literature where there are no strictly defined "right" answers, impression marking plays a big part in determining your final grade. So you not only have to turn up, but you also have to stay awake. And for maximum effect, keep your eyes wide open and ask intelligent sounding questions like "What is the relevance of this novel in our everyday lives?"

✦ **Establish broadband, high-speed lines of communication.** Decipher the messages your teachers are sending, and analyse their style of communication. For example, you might realise some teachers like to preface certain points with cue phrases like "Pay attention to the following" or "This is really important" to indicate that what they are about to teach is essential information and will be appearing in the next test. Don't miss these clues! At the same time, you also want to give your teacher some feedback on how well you understand the material so he or she can adjust the way the material is taught.

✦ **Process the message for useful information.** The key point here is that you have to use your judgement to decide if a piece of information is important or not. Teachers make mistakes, and you do not want to confuse yourself further by learning these mistakes. When you feel there is a contradiction in meaning the best thing to do is to clarify it with the teacher. You can also check it using different sources, such as your textbook or the Internet.

✦ **Respect them and show appreciation for what they do.** When I was a student I often behaved in a rude and disrespectful way to my teachers – by sleeping in class, doing my own thing or yawning loudly. I paid for this inappropriate behaviour by the resulting poor relationship with some of my teachers. Showing them appreciation is really up to the individual, but you could at least throw in a kind word on Alien Benefactors Day, which falls on the first day of the ninth month of every human year.

Learning from multiple sources

Nobody can teach you anything; you can only learn it yourself. You have to do the work. But teachers can assist in making the learning process easier and more digestible. They can inspire you and ignite your interest in the subject.

Keep an open but filtered mind. Be sceptical about what you are taught, and take the initiative to find out the truth for yourself. No topic can be understood thoroughly from just one source – not your teacher, not the textbook, not even an encyclopaedia. Gain a deeper understanding of the topic by learning it from multiple sources. These include your teachers, newspapers, magazine articles, books, other textbooks, the Internet and even cartoon and beginners books. Do not be ashamed to start from the simplest source to grasp the fundamentals of a topic. It's a great way to start.

Personally I find it a painful chore to memorise something by reading it over and over again. By learning from many sources, you will also remember your information in a more comprehensive way without the need to sit down and memorise it.

Be careful which sources you learn from. Some guidebooks and even textbooks are filled with factual mistakes. You could end up learning the wrong thing, which will not only confuse you but will also prove difficult to unlearn. Stick to respected publishers of educational material. Be a connoisseur – selective and discriminating – in your choice of study material.

Teachers have to take on the critical and sometimes dreadful task of educating a classroom-full of highly resistant individuals. As much as you detest the mountains of homework they pile on you, the sharp nasal whine and dictatorial style of the discipline mistress, or the blatant favouritism shown by your form teacher, give them a break. While they might act alien, they're really human too.

ACING THOSE PESKY EXAMS

Exams are a necessary but unfortunate inconvenience of your schooling experience. They are meant to test your understanding of the subject matter, to give educators a way to judge how well you know your stuff, and as a prod to motivate you to study.

Let's be frank – exams are important. How well you do determines what classes you take, your chances to enter a university, and eventually the jobs you can get. They affect what people/society/parents/friends think of you, and also what you think of yourself.

The techniques I am about to share with you will help you prepare for this duel, including the training you need, the approach to take and pointers for the showdown.

The run-up

Anywhere between one week to three months before the big test or exam, start to get serious about your review. The most important thing is to plan your time properly:

- List out all topics in all subjects you will be tested on.
- Estimate how much time you need to cover an average topic. Double that estimate (you always take longer than you think).
- Assign a specific date and time to every topic you are going to cover, in forty-five minute to one-hour chunks (the maximum period the average brain can take before fatigue affects your absorption of the material). For example, if you estimate you need two hours to complete the topic "The Properties of Matter", split it into two parts of one hour each.
- Ideally, you would have enough time to cover your material at least thrice. Your first run through the material is to give you a feel for it – you won't remember much. Your second run through will allow you to focus on the important points and commit them to memory. Your third run through is to review the material, ensuring you have not missed out or forgotten anything, and to "lock in" that knowledge.

✦   Remember to schedule in brief breaks (from five to fifteen minutes each) between your hour-long sessions and to include the occasional longer break (thirty minutes to an hour) to go for a walk, read your email, de-stress on a computer game or chat with a friend.

Your goal should be to cover the material so thoroughly you are confident that no matter what questions come up on the exam, you will be able to answer them. And if you can't, nobody else who has studied the same material can. The keyword here is *confidence*.

This sounds intimidating. How can you ever expect to know enough about your topic to answer any question that comes up on it (as long as it tests material within the syllabus)?

First, take a question-oriented approach to studying the material. This involves asking questions about it from every possible angle. Check all the past year questions you can get your hands on, look in textbooks for end-of-chapter review questions, and even brainstorm some of your own.

Next, find the answers to these questions. If you come up with the questions before you do your second or third runs through the subject, you will be subconsciously focusing your mind to look for the answers. Your study time will be much more purposeful and productive because your mind has a goal.

One thing you'll notice when compiling questions from all sorts of different sources is the great degree of overlap in the kinds of questions that can be asked about any one topic. That's where your confidence for taking the exam will come from, as you know that the mass of questions coming out will be familiar to you. And if you prepared well, you'll even be able to tackle the occasional trick question or two.

Make sure the answers you have prepared are accurate and comprehensive. You are aiming to get full marks if the exact same question appears in the exam. That'll give you a lot of leeway to screw up and make careless mistakes elsewhere, and takes a lot of pressure off you. You want to build up your confidence to the point where you feel that no matter what, you will do well (at least on a relative basis).

More pointers to help you store the information in your head for optimum recall:

✦ **Make extensive use of memory aids (e.g. mnemonic devices).** For example, I used the acronym ABCD earlier in this book to help you remember the four traits mature people possess (according to Dr. M. Scott Peck), namely that they i) **A**ccept responsibility for their lives ii) **B**alance the different parts of their lives iii) **C**onsciously live and iv) **D**elay gratification.

✦ **Summarise your notes as much as possible.** Only include key words and essential points, and use short forms you are familiar with. Aim to summarise the entire topic onto one sheet of paper, and test yourself to see if you can "expand" it back out. Talk yourself through the whole process. If you can thoroughly explain a concept to someone else without referring to your notes, you know your stuff.

✦ **Involve as many senses as you can.** For example, if you are trying to remember the Water Cycle, visualise the evaporation of water molecules from a body of water. See them rising through the air. Feel their increasing density as the temperature drops. See how they condense into clouds when they cannot remain as vapour anymore. Imagine you are flying through a fluffy cloud, which has been growing until it gets too heavy and the water droplets start to precipitate and fall back to the earth. Smell the rain, see the lightning from the storm and hear the roaring thunder. If it's like a scene from a movie, you'll find it hard to forget. If you want, make the images naughty or shocking. Too outrageous for you? Great, you'll remember it even better.

There is much more to learn about using your memory, good study strategies and tools to optimise your learning efforts, but it would take a whole other book (or two) to cover these. Mastering these techniques will allow you to become more efficient with your studying, and free up time for you to do your own things.

My own motto: **Maximum learning with minimum effort**.

If you have diligently planned your time, compiled lots of questions about the material, and found and learnt the answers to those, then you should have few problems during ...

The showdown

Relax, you have done all you can to prepare for this exam. Rest well the night before. There is no point pulling an all-nighter. It will cost you the concentration and mental agility you need to ace the exam.

Once the exam begins, do not cave in to the pressure to start answering questions immediately. Spend a minute flipping through the exam paper to get a feel of the questions and to make a mental allotment of the time you need to spend on the various sections. This is to ensure you have enough time to make a decent attempt at each question. Good time management is essential – you do not want to be in a situation where the time is up and you have easy questions left blank.

Once you begin, DON'T STOP! No matter what, plough your way through the whole exam. Using a watch to pace yourself, move steadily from question to question. If you get stuck on one and have no idea how to answer it, move on. It doesn't matter, you should know enough to answer the rest of the questions and get a good grade.

If you finish before the time is up, resist the temptation to leave the classroom or to sleep. This is precious exam time you're using, and your only chance to go back and check your answers. Go through everything again, looking out for careless mistakes.

Time's up! Hand in your paper, get out of the classroom and breathe some fresh air. There's not much point discussing the paper with your classmates, as you'll only fret about the questions you didn't answer correctly. Oh, and if anybody asks how you did for the exam, just smile and say, "Okay."

The spoils of your victory

However you actually did for the exam, you know the results are much better than it would have been if you did not properly prepare for it. Give yourself a pat on the back.

It's human nature, but try not to compare yourself with others. There'll always be people who did better than you, and people who did worse. The only person you're competing against is yourself.

The study method I have outlined above is one that should see you through a test or exam on any subject. It worked for me, but you have to decide whether it's right for you. If something else works better, go ahead and do it.

I believe the three most important steps in any strategy for learning are: i) Asking questions, ii) Making your own notes and iii) Review. Asking questions keeps you mindful of what you are studying and helps you make sense of the subject. Making your own notes and summarizing them is a good way to make the knowledge your own. Very few people on the face of this earth have a photographic memory. In order to remember well, you have to review the material more than once.

One caveat is that this method is geared towards acing exams. It does not necessarily encourage a passion for learning or a desire to gain knowledge for its own sake. Its focus is to get you the best possible grades, because exams are crucial in determining the future opportunities available to you.

I do not want you to get trapped in the mindset of "finding the right answer". I once tutored a primary school girl in Mathematics. It frustrated me to discover she cared less for the process of learning than for getting the "right answer". She only cared that the answer was "2566" (even if she had to peek at the answers at the back of the textbook).

My fear is you will become so result-oriented and focused on grades that you become unwilling to spend time to understand what you are learning and its relevance to the real world, and thus unable to find pleasure in the process.

MAKING THE MOST OF SCHOOL

> I never let schooling interfere with my education.
> – *Mark Twain*

What does the word "education" mean to you? Is it:

1. An endless battery of tests to ensure you've memorised a whole encyclopaedia's worth of trivia?
2. Instilling a deep fear of authority in you by threatening dire consequences for your disobedience?
3. Training you to repeat information mindlessly until it sinks in?

To me it is option four: Inculcating a love of knowledge and learning, and equipping you with the skills you need to lead a thoughtful, productive and meaningful life.

What are the traits of an educated person? Here is my personal opinion on the four traits an educated person should have:

1. He knows a bit about a lot of things and a lot about a few things
2. He is able to think critically and reach his own independent conclusions
3. He is a master of the skills of learning
4. He is able to communicate effectively, in both speech and writing

Are you receiving an education that develops these traits in you?

1) He knows a bit about a lot of things and a lot about a few things

I hope you get to choose what you want to study based on your strengths and interests. Often, you are pressured into choosing something you do not like or have little aptitude for. From a young age you are expected to know which path you want to take and what you want to specialize in.

There are many things you should know about but are not likely to learn in school, subjects that are essential to your well-being and livelihood – basic financial management, etiquette and social skills, home economics and "handyman" skills, and an awareness of global issues and problems. These "lifeskills" are necessary for you to become an independent, responsible and graceful citizen of the world. Chances are, nobody's going to teach you all these things at school. If they don't teach you, learn it yourself! Take the initiative to create your own curriculum to fill in any gaps in your education. These lessons can be learnt by reading, taking a relevant course or by wisely choosing the student groups you join.

2) He is able to think critically and reach his own independent conclusions

Effective thinking involves a weighing of all available evidence and unabashedly questioning the prevailing "truths".

> What is the hardest task in the world? To think.
> – *Ralph Waldo Emerson*

We are often dependent on spoon-feeding to get the correct answer. Rather than letting us figure things out for ourselves and risk us not learning the correct information, it is served on a silver platter. There is no need to think. The answers are there, just learn it up. If faced with a choice between memorizing a sheet of correct answers and having to go out and assemble your own (which may or may not be correct), you'd probably think: Why bother?

But when faced with a new and unfamiliar situation, you'd be at a loss because you have not learnt the process of analyzing it. Thinking is a set of skills, not a quick fix.

Weaning ourselves off spoon-feeding is a difficult task. Spoon-feeding is like a drug. We get angry, upset and eventually desperate without it. I remember the laborious explanations my Physics teacher would go into when explaining the intricacies of a tricky question, and myself thinking, "Just give me the ANSWER, darn it!" We want the drug, and ignore its ill effects.

What can be done to kick the habit? Start processing information from a range of sources – books, current affairs programs, magazine articles and textbooks. Study the arguments and the reasoning used. Be a sceptic – question everything.

3)   He is a master of the skills of learning

Learning how to learn is such a fundamental skill it is outrageous that virtually no student is taught it. The reasons for this, in my opinion, are twofold: Firstly, learning is thought to be a natural process ("no one needs to be taught how to learn"). Secondly, learning is thought to be more a matter of effort than technique. If you sit the student down and coerce him to repeat the material a number of times (a multiple dependant on his natural intelligence), he will learn. It does not matter how he assimilates that material.

These mindsets have been found to be inaccurate by many learning gurus. Yes, learning is a natural process, but there are optimal ways to learn, and these ways are sometimes different from the traditional methods. For example, the predominant method in which ideas are organised is the Linear Method. Ideas run on in phrases, sentences and paragraphs from left to right, top of the page to the bottom. With his invention of Mind Mapping, Tony Buzan has introduced a completely different way of organizing information, with associations and images being more important than a standard linear format.

Tests have been carried out where two identical groups of students are given the same material to study. One group was taught and instructed to use various learning enhancement techniques such as Mind Mapping, previewing or goal setting. The other group was given no special instructions. A test on the material was then given. In all cases the former group outperformed the latter group. The way you learn makes a significant difference in how well you learn.

These skills of learning are applied at four different parts of the process: Locating the information (research and library skills), processing the information (reading and thinking skills), integrating the information into your knowledge base and recalling the information successfully (memory skills).

Be an independent learner. Do not be afraid to explore and experiment to find what works for you.

4)   He is able to communicate effectively

You have all these great ideas in your head, but how do you get them across to another person? That's what effective communication is about. How far you get in life is heavily dependent on your proficiency in this area – there is no point having brilliant ideas if people do not understand you.

Writing well is more than just being able to use fancy vocabulary. It is about using language in a simple yet powerful way to carry your message. How to write well? Write often and learn the ropes. I believe in "reading osmosis" – you have to read examples of fine writing to learn.

Language lessons and essay writing are a staple of our curriculum, but learning to speak well is not. Speaking well means that your voice, diction, pacing and dynamics all enhance rather than detract from your message.

Life skills

The primary aim of the formal schooling system is to ensure every child who passes through becomes functionally literate and numerate, more simply expressed as the three "Rs" of education – "Reading, writing and arithmetic". These are the core foundational skills every person needs to be productive and to participate in modern society.

However, there are other skills you might never learn during your schooling experience that are equally essential for you to lead an effective and successful life. Some people have even managed to rise to the top of their professions without being literate or numerate based on their exceptional strengths in one or more of these skills.

The skills you need to pick up to prepare yourself for a surefooted entry into the adult world include:

✦ **People skills.** Whether it be for making friends, working as part of a team or managing and leading others, people skills are perhaps the most important skills to learn. We will suffer if we cannot get along with other people. Our success and happiness in life is primarily determined by our relationship with the people around us. The Jewish rabbis knew this centuries ago when they taught, simply, that life is with people.

✦ **Communication skills.** Requiring a combination of literacy and people skills, communication skills enable you to effectively express your ideas to others. Your linguistic ability, proficiency at public speaking and the elegance of your writing are all things you can work on.

◆ **Self-management skills.** Worthwhile achievements come as a result of discipline, productive use of time and the discerning utilization of resources. Knowing what goals to aim for requires you to look deep within to identify your values, strengths and weaknesses. Learning to manage your time properly will help you overcome procrastination and focus your efforts towards reaching your goals. Learning to manage your finances – to save and to invest – will help you build wealth and abundance in your future. Much of self-management is about sacrificing what gives you pleasure now to reap a bigger and more lasting payoff in the future, i.e. delaying gratification.

◆ **Quality of Life skills.** Life is not just about getting good grades in school and then earning lots of money when you work. Learning to play a sport or a musical instrument; learning to appreciate art, literature and theatre; and learning to share your knowledge and time with others will enrich your life immeasurably. Learn to enjoy life.

◆ **Productivity skills.** Unless you are the recipient of a large inheritance you will have to make your living by providing products or services somebody is willing to pay you for. Knowing how to use a computer is a vital requirement for almost every job available in an office setting. Learning how to use a word processor to create professional looking documents, learning to touch type to leverage your ability to input data, and learning to search the Internet for the information you need are all a must.

Although your school might not directly teach you these things, opportunities abound for you to learn and practise these skills. Your student groups or the activities you are involved in give you a channel through which to practise your people, communication and quality of life skills. Balancing your academic and personal life successfully will require you to exercise your self-management and productivity skills to the fullest.

Getting a real education

> If a person masters the fundamentals of his subject and has learned to think independently, he will surely find his way and besides will better adapt himself to progress and changes than the person whose training consists principally in the acquiring of detailed knowledge.
>
> *– Albert Einstein*

If you think your education is something you can only get at school, something your teachers have to drill into you or to serve you on a silver platter, it's time to change your mindset.

Your education is in your hands. Some people go to school and even to university and don't learn anything. Others learn the most valuable lessons in their life outside of school. Some people drift aimlessly through their youth, picking up whatever sticks. Others choose to learn and practice things they are interested in, or things they think will be useful to them later in life. All of them have made a choice. Even doing nothing is a choice. You can choose to create your own syllabus of subjects and skills to learn, or you can choose to while away your time watching television and playing computer games.

Aim to do your best at school. Is it not better to succeed within the system while filling the gaps in your education at the same time, than to rebel and get locked out of so many opportunities? Furthermore, numeracy and literacy are essential skills that enable you to pick up new knowledge.

> Every man who knows how to read has it in his power to magnify himself, to multiply the ways in which he exists, to make his life full, significant, and interesting.
>
> *– Aldous Huxley*

Learning takes effort. You can have the best notes, textbooks and teachers, but to ever gain any new knowledge, you have to personally engage with the material. If only we could download data from the Internet and record it in our brains like a hard disk, retrieving it whenever we need the information. But we can't.

Reading widely will give you a breadth and depth of knowledge and understanding that will add to and surpass what you learn in school. The library is your greatest resource. It has a wide selection of books for you to choose from and it's free.

English is the language via which most of your subjects are taught, and it is also the international language of business. A good command of English is an enormous advantage in learning and doing well in any subject taught in the language, especially in the humanities such as Literature, History and Geography. It is an advantage even in subjects like Mathematics, where the wordy problem sums challenge those who are weak in English.

Language is best learned by immersion. Your goal should be the ability to think fluently in the language. The rules of grammar are important, but more important is getting a feel and an instinct for the language. Immerse yourself in exemplary examples of the language. Reading books by fluent authors, listening to the radio and participating in debates are all ways to improve your proficiency.

Do not neglect your mother tongue, for it is your connection to your culture and may prove invaluable in work and business later in life. I wish I had put more effort into learning Mandarin during my primary and secondary school days.

Participate actively in student groups and activities of your choice. Take up courses or join clubs to learn new things. The time you invest will give you huge returns.

Part 6
A Life Worth Living

Brief Contents

DANCING ON A TIGHTROPE

> We have all experienced times when, instead of being buffeted by anonymous forces, we do feel in control of our actions, masters of our own fate. On the rare occasions that it happens, we feel a sense of exhilaration, a deep sense of enjoyment that is long cherished and that becomes a landmark in memory for what life should be like. This is what we mean by optimal experience.
>
> *– Mihaly Csikszentmihalyi*

For thirty years Professor Mihaly Csikszentmihalyi (pronounced "chick-sent-me-high-ee") has been researching optimal experience. He found the key to moments of fulfilling absorption to be a state of consciousness called "flow" – a feeling as though one were carried along by waves; a feeling of complete immersion.

Flow is not confined to any particular activity, whether work or leisure – even the dullest routine can become a flow activity. When I was twelve my class was made to spring clean our classroom at the end of the school year, which included mopping the floor, cleaning the windows and wiping all the tables and chairs. Considering most of us never lifted a finger to help out with the chores at home, and how we hated sweeping the floor or wiping the whiteboard during our classroom duties, we were not looking forward to it.

On the day of the spring cleaning (a Saturday no less), quite a few people did not even turn up. Reluctantly and with a great sense of tedium, we began the chore of returning our classroom to its pristine state before our subsequent "contamination". Then something strange happened – someone splashed water onto the floor instead of mopping it, and people started to slide across the floor as though they were surfing. It was like a game, and with no teachers around to supervise us, we started to compete in all sorts of cleaning competitions. We even vied for the right to use the mop or to splash water onto the floor! We had so much fun, by the time we were done, we had unknowingly spent a couple of hours cleaning our classroom.

> People who learn to control inner experience will be able to determine the quality of their lives, which is as close as any of us can come to being happy.
>
> – *Mihaly Csikszentmihalyi*

Flow activities must pose a sufficient level of challenge to your skills. If the activity is not challenging enough you feel bored; if it is too difficult, you feel overwhelmed. Of course, some activities are more amenable to flow than others, but with an understanding of the conditions that lead to flow experiences, we can derive a greater amount of enjoyment from life.

Achieving flow

> Contrary to expectation, "flow" usually happens not during relaxing moments of leisure and entertainment, but rather when we are actively involved in a difficult enterprise, in a task that stretches our mental and physical abilities.
>
> – *Mihaly Csikszentmihalyi*

To experience flow Professor Csikszentmihalyi suggests picking an activity that is enjoyable to you and is at, or slightly above, your skill level. As your performance improves, continually "raise the bar" by making the activity more difficult. Screen out any distractions so you can focus your attention on the activity. Set concrete goals to help monitor your progress and to get feedback on performance.

Athletes are one of the most prominent examples of flow in action. They continually push themselves to improve their times, distances or shots. They have concrete goals to reach, in terms of their performance and in competition rankings. It is no wonder athletes often describe experiencing a sense of euphoria, of "being in the moment".

Playing a musical instrument is often a "flowful" activity as well. As the musician's skills improve, he or she attempts more difficult pieces or learns more advanced techniques. The sheer auditory beauty of music combined with the challenge of mastering an instrument makes music a pleasurable pursuit.

Learning can be a flow activity as well. There is a thrill in finding out things you never knew before, in attaining a greater depth of understanding of a topic, and in seeing the world in new ways. Clear goals as to how much you want to learn can be set. You have control over your foray into new areas of knowledge, and you can test yourself to obtain feedback on how well you are learning.

Unfortunately, most students have little control over what they learn in school. There are rigid syllabi that must be followed and little chance for the individual student to explore his or her own interests. The level of challenge is tuned for the "average student", and thus the slower students feel lost while the capable students are bored.

One way of dealing with this is to treat learning like a game. Establish your objectives (why you have to study this subject), the challenges to be overcome (what you have to learn), your own goals (how well you want to do) and the rewards (the prize you get if you reach your goals).

> It turns out that watching TV is not at all a flowful activity. People generally report higher levels of stress, depression, and tension after watching TV. It seems that TV's main virtue is that it occupies the mind undemandingly. Flow is hard to achieve without effort. Flow is not "wasting time".
>
> – *Mihaly Csikszentmihalyi*

Most people watch TV mindlessly. They watch it to fill up the pocket of time they have between dinner and sleep to help them relax. Watching TV is not bad per se, it just depends on what you're getting out of it. This applies to computers as well, which are more amenable to the experience of flow. Hunting down information or coding your own web pages or computer programs can be engrossing activities. But computers can also be used for mindless activities that may be momentarily entertaining but have no lasting value.

Flow is not a drug that strings your life into a series of psychedelic highs. Life is, and will be, sometimes mundane and routine. But gaining an understanding of flow will help enhance your day-to day experiences and inspire you to try new activities.

The great balancing act

We need balance. Would you be happy to be brilliant academically but friendless? A holistic approach to living addresses imbalances by getting you to pay attention to the different important areas in your life.

While you're still in school and not yet financially independent, the main areas you need to cultivate are your:

- **Mind.** No scientist has been able to find a limit to the potential of the human brain – it is believed most human beings use less than a tiny fraction of their brain's potential. How much are you using?
- **Body.** How well have you been taking care of your body? Without your health you cannot enjoy what life has to offer. Are you eating nutritious food? Are you limiting your intake of nicotine, alcohol or other harmful substances? Are you exercising regularly in order to develop strength, agility and endurance?
- **Spirit.** This is the essence of who you are, the "inner you" or your "heart". How much joy, love and inspiration do you have in your life? How much do you share with others? What are your dreams? Have you been nurturing them? Have you been setting time aside to reflect and contemplate on life and how you've been living it?
- **Skills.** What are you good at? What do you need to be good at? How developed are those skills?
- **Academics.** School is the major focus of the early stage of your life. How much you learn and how well you do at school are separate but closely related things – the difference is how good you are at communicating what you know. Do you attend lessons regularly? Pay attention in class? Do your homework? Learn from your mistakes?
- **Family.** Whatever your relationship with them, you share an undeniable genetic bond with your family.
- **Friends.** You have different types of friends, differing in terms of the level of intimacy and situation – best buddies, casual acquaintances and activity partners. Each type of friend has a place

in a full and balanced social network. Have you been spending time developing your social network?

Knowing what is good for you is not the same as actually doing it. There are no instant or overnight solutions. The purpose of this framework is to make you aware of the changes you need to make to restore balance in your life. We often coast mindlessly until a crisis (failing an exam, suicidal feelings, a health problem) jolts us into realizing we've been ignoring a particular area for too long. It is only when you are aware of a problem that you can do something about it.

ACHIEVING YOUR DREAMS

> If one advances confidently in the direction of his dreams, and endeavours to live the life which he has imagined, he will meet with a success unexpected in common hours.
>
> — *Henry David Thoreau*

A dream is a vision you have of what you want. To achieve it you first translate it into a set of goals, then into a plan for action. Most people have dreams but only a few build the bridge through to reality.

Dreams do not have to be large and impressive. They could be anything from being able to speak Japanese to learning how to salsa.

Do you think accomplishing "big" things in your life is impossible? As Henry Ford said, "Whether you think you can or can't, you're right." If someone else has done it before, you can do it too. If no one has but you think you can, go ahead and give it your best shot.

Finding your passion

> The desire not to be anything is the desire not to be.
>
> — *Ayn Rand*

What if you don't know what your dreams are? How do you figure them out? Think back to the times when you used phrases like "I wish I...", "If only I could..." or "Wouldn't it be great if I..." What do your thoughts and words show? Catching these flitting thoughts is a bit like catching butterflies. Be ready with your net at all times, on the lookout for that elusive creature.

What inspires you? Excites you? Grips your imagination? If you could do or become anything you wanted to, what would it be? Cast aside your self-doubts and perceived limitations for a moment – leave "but I can't" or "there's no way I could" at the door.

Take your time. Finding your passion is not an overnight process for most people. It could take weeks or months or even years. The important thing is to ask the questions now, plant the seeds in your mind, and start to watch and observe yourself. What do you gravitate to? What gives you a rush of excitement? What can you spend hours doing without noticing time passing?

Once you catch on to a dream, write it down, think about it, keep it alive. It's important not to let your dreams fizzle out and die. Becoming an author is one of my dreams. When I first told friends I wanted to write a book, some were doubtful ("Ha ha!"), while others were somewhat more encouraging ("You? Write a book? Ha ha!").

But by far the biggest doubter of all was myself. What made me think I had anything useful to say? What if my writing sucked and was not funny or interesting? What if people laughed at me and said, "What a pathetic attempt! We always knew you were no good"? Don't let anyone smother your dreams, but watch out especially for your own doubts and insecurities. They are often your worst enemies.

Accomplishing your goals

To span the gap between a dream and its realization, you need to turn it into something more concrete – a goal.

Goals are the purpose toward which an endeavour is directed – an objective, a mission. Goals need to be specific, detailed and sufficiently ambitious to inspire you, to make you stretch and reach for the stars just outside your grasp. The goal that led to this book was "I want to write a book for young people and share what I've learnt about life."

Goals are flexible. They can be continually tweaked and adjusted as you discover what works for you and what doesn't. It's a process of finding the best method to get from where you are to where you want to go. At first I thought of writing a novel. I came up with a plot, list of characters and themes for the story, and started writing a few chapters. Then I realised a non-fiction format for my book would be more appropriate for what I had to say, and so I took out a blank sheet of paper and started planning again.

Goals need not be an end-point. They can be a road marker to other goals as well. Now that I've written this book, I might go back and finish the story I started writing. I also have an idea for another book. It's like a chain reaction. Once you start putting your dreams into action you get more and more ideas. The difficult part is the starting.

Step 1 – Write your goals down

Take a blank sheet of paper, and write down in as much detail as possible what you want to achieve and why you want to achieve it. Once you write it down, it is no longer in the murky recesses of your mind but in black and white right before your eyes.

For this book I wrote down: "I want to write a book for young people, sharing the lessons I have learnt on how to live fully. It will include sections on self-esteem, friendship, relationships, school and achieving your goals. I want to write it because I feel I have something of value to share and have the ability to do it. I enjoy writing, and would enjoy my status as an author." It's all down there – a clear direction to head in and compelling reasons to make the journey.

Write down all the goals you wish to accomplish, regardless of how small or impossible you think they are. Brainstorm and be specific – what exactly do you want to achieve? Do you want to "do well" in your mathematics exam or get an A for it?

We'll be using Joe, our new imaginary friend, as an example to help illustrate some of these steps. Here is what Joe has written down as the goals he wants to achieve:

Goals	Details
Start a blog	Include links to favourite sites and also pictures of friends and family
Get an A for Chinese Language	Raise my grade in Chinese from C to A
Organise a post-exam party for classmates	A BBQ by the beach would be nice
Learn to play the guitar	Be able to strum and sing simple songs, then see whether I am interested to go further
Learn to play tennis	Find a tennis coach at a sports club and learn how to play
Write a short story to enter in a competition	Maximum 1500 words, must have family values as the theme

Step 2 – Give each goal a time frame and priority

Next, give each goal a time frame. How long will it take to accomplish? If it is a large goal, what intermediate steps will you need to achieve and how long will those take?

Now assign a priority to each goal based on your current interests, available resources and level of confidence. If you had to choose, which one would you do first? Give that goal a 1, then ask yourself which one you would do next, and give that goal a 2. You don't necessarily have to work on only one goal at a time, but prioritising your goals will let you focus on the ones that are most important to you.

Below is an example of our imaginary friend Joe's goals. You can download free blank copies of these forms for your own use at the Aktive Learning website (www.aktive.com.sg).

Priority	Goals	Details	Time needed
2	Start a blog	Include links to favourite sites and also pictures of friends and family	1 week
1	Get an A for Chinese	Raise my grade in Chinese from C to A	1 year
3	Organise a post-exam party for classmates	A BBQ by the beach would be nice	1 month
6	Learn to play the guitar	Be able to strum and sing simple songs, then see whether I am interested to go further	6 months
5	Learn to play tennis	Find a tennis coach at a sports club and learn how to play	3 months
4	Write a short story to enter in a competition	Maximum 1500 words, must have family values as the theme	1 week

Step 3 – Analyse your goals

Now that you have your goals written down, it's time to formulate your game plan – specific steps you must take to accomplish your goal. Ask yourself: What do I need to do? Do I currently have the skills and resources needed to tackle this goal?

If you want to write a book, a prerequisite would be a good command of the language you want to write it in. Do you have that now? Or should you spend some time brushing up your grammar and vocabulary first?

Break a large goal into many small steps – this is your action plan. You will begin to see how you can accomplish what once seemed to be an unreachable target.

As an example, my action plan for writing this book was:

1)	Brainstorm subject and contents	1 week
2)	Organise and come up with contents page	1 week
3)	Reading and research	3 months
4)	Write first draft	6 months
5)	Editing, polishing and more research	2 months
6)	Send second draft for external editing	1 month
7)	Prepare final manuscript	2 weeks

I assigned specific deadlines to each step, not just as a gauge to see how long the whole process would take, but also to keep up the pressure and motivation to reach my goal.

Because writing a book is such a large project, I had to break these steps down into even smaller micro-steps, things that I could do right now to get started (e.g. "Think of ten topics young people are concerned about").

Think about the steps you need to take to help you reach each of your goals in the most effective way. See below for an example of Joe's progress at this stage for his top three goals:

Priority	Goals	Steps
1	Get an A for Chinese	1) Find out schedule for Chinese classes at a language school and sign up for it
		2) Listen to Chinese radio every morning during breakfast
		3) Learn five new words a day from the vocabulary book
		4) Look up dictionary for meaning of words I come across but do not understand
		5) Read a Chinese news website for thirty minutes a day
2	Start a blog	1) Research different blogging websites and choose one to use
		2) Register at a blogging website and write my first post
3	Organise a post-exam party for classmates	1) Create a form to pass around and find out what days classmates are free
		2) Get phone number to book BBQ pits and book one on best date
		3) Find out what sort of supplies to buy and what sort of food people want and make a list
		4) Collect money from classmates to pay for food and supplies
		5) Get a few friends to help buy and carry supplies to the BBQ pit

Step 4 – Commit yourself by setting a deadline

Next to each step you have outlined, write down the expected frequency (if it's something you'll have to do regularly, e.g. "Jog on Mondays and Thursdays") or deadline (if it's a one-off thing, e.g. "Call up tuition centre to find out about courses"). Don't try to do too much at one time. Be realistic and take things slow at first, giving yourself more than enough time to carry out each step. The important thing is to do a little bit every day to create momentum.

Priority	Goals	Steps	Start date	Deadline/ Frequency
1	Get an A for Chinese Language	1) Find out schedules for Chinese classes at a language school and sign up for it	Apr 10	Weekly
		2) Listen to Chinese radio every morning during breakfast	Apr 10	Daily
		3) Learn five new words a day from the vocabulary book	Apr 10	Daily
		4) Look up dictionary for meaning of words I come across but do not understand	Apr 10	Whenever
		5) Read a Chinese news website for thirty minutes a day	Apr 10	Daily
2	Start a blog	1) Research different blogging websites and choose one to use	Apr 10	Apr 11
		2) Register at a blogging website and write my first post	Apr 12	Apr 12
3	Organise a post-exam party for classmates	1) Create a form to pass around and find out what days classmates are free	Apr 11	Apr 12
		2) Get phone number to book BBQ pits and book one on best date	Apr 13	Apr 13
		3) Find out what sort of supplies to buy and what sort of food people want and make a list	Apr 14	Apr 20
		4) Collect money from classmates to pay for food and supplies	May 18	May 19
		5) Get a few friends to help buy and carry supplies to the BBQ pit	May 23	May 23

Guess what? We have just completed a goal setting exercise!

If previously you only had a vague notion of what your goals were and how to reach them, after going through these first four steps you now have it down in detail. Make sure the goals you set have these three features:

1. A priority
2. Detail – what specific actions you need to take
3. A deadline

Step 5 – Do it

As the old proverb goes: "A journey of ten thousand miles begins with a single step." Plank by plank by plank you build your bridge from dream to reality. It's as simple as this: Figure out what you have to do, then do it. It's not easy, but it's simple.

THE DREAM KILLERS

Most people never see their dreams become reality. They get stuck, lose their momentum or nerve, and stop trying. As you progress towards your goals you will inevitably face the Dream Killers – fearsome monsters who suck the marrow out of your dreams.

Dream Killer #1 – Procrastination

Procrastination is the granddaddy of Dream Killers. If you put off doing something you ought to have done today, you are procrastinating. When you procrastinate, you are letting time slip through your hands like sand while the things you need to do pile up. There are numerous reasons why people procrastinate, including:

+ **Laziness/lethargy/inertia.** "But I don't have the energy! I'm too tired!" The paradox about energy is – the less you use it, the less you have. I often used "I'm too tired" as an excuse not to exercise. But once I forced myself to exercise I began to feel more energised and alive.
+ **Ignorance.** "But I don't know how!" If you have no idea what to do, you will do nothing.
+ **A sense of helplessness.** "I just can't do it, nothing I do makes a difference." You feel you have no control over your life and it is futile doing anything about it.
+ **Fear of failure.** You don't try because you believe you will fail, and you dread the accompanying feelings of inadequacy. You take failure personally. When you make a mistake, you don't say: "I made a mistake on that one"; you say: "I'm a failure."
+ **Fear of success.** Sounds counter-intuitive, but some people are afraid of actually succeeding at their goals, because their lives will change drastically. The discomfort involved in change is greater than the familiar suffering of their current situation.
+ **Limiting beliefs.** "It's impossible, no one can do it." That's what people thought about running the mile (approximately 1.6 kilometres) under four minutes until 1954, when Sir Roger Bannister

broke through this mental barrier. He had done it not only by intense physical training, but also by convincing himself that it was possible and by mentally rehearsing the run many times in his head. The interesting thing is, the year after he broke the "impossible" barrier at Oxford, thirty-seven other runners broke it. And the next year, another three hundred did it! Only when they saw it could be done did they believe they could do it too.

> Procrastination is the art of keeping up with yesterday
> – Don Marquis

What can be done to overcome procrastination?

Remember the experiment I asked you to try in the Introduction where you had to stare at a clock for three minutes, focus your thoughts on it and try to feel enthusiastic about the task? It's hard to boss your feelings around, and thoughts are difficult to control. Only your actions are largely under your control.

Think back to a time you were successful – you won a medal in a competition, did well for a test or managed to get a date with this guy or girl you liked. No problems thinking or feeling positively there right? In fact, you felt great!

With references of success (records of instances where you succeeded), it is easier to think and feel positive. The action came first, and then the thoughts and feelings followed. Instead of waiting till you feel like doing something productive, take action to create more references of success for yourself. The more you succeed, the easier it is to convince yourself you will be successful the next time.

The key is to accept whatever feelings you may be having and then do what you have to do anyway. For the negative thoughts that cross your mind it helps to argue with them. It sounds crazy but it works. Argue back with the voice of reason:

Your mind: I'll never make it.

You: You haven't tried so how do you know?

Your mind: I've always been a failure. Why should this time be different?

You: You have not always been a failure. Remember the time you aced that test? Or the time you won a prize in the competition?

Your mind: But this is different. I know I'll fail.

You: You never know until you try. And the only way to find out is to try.

So you argue with the irrational negative thoughts in your mind, systematically refuting every objection that comes along until you reach: "You never know until you try. And the only way to find out is to try."

Dream Killer #2 – Failure

Okay, you did it. You tried. But you fell face down and made a loud splat. You were tripped by Failure. Now what?

> Ever tried. Ever failed. No matter. Try Again. Fail again. Fail better.
>
> *– Samuel Beckett*

There is a story about Sir Winston Churchill, the British Prime Minister who led his country courageously during World War II. He was scheduled to make a speech at an elementary school. He was known to be a great orator, and the auditorium was packed with students and teachers who wanted to hear him speak. At the appointed time Churchill strolled onto the stage and towards the podium. A hush of silence fell onto the crowd, out of respect and in anticipation of a brilliant speech. When he reached the podium Churchill remained silent for a long time before he said, "Never, never, never, never, never, never give up." Then he turned around and walked off the stage.

Take failure as feedback. Learn from it. Bounce back. Next time you'll do better.

Dream Killer #3 – Parental Objections

What do you do if your parents disapprove, or worse, outright object to your plans? This is a tricky problem. You owe your existence and your upbringing to your parents, but your life and your actions are your own. Your parents often want the best for you and they think they know what that is. They are often correct, but there are times when you know what is best for yourself.

> How selfhood begins with a walking away,
> And love is proved in the letting go.
> – *C. Day Lewis*

Think hard: What is the reason for their objections? Are they object-ing to your choices out of your best interests or out of their own fears? It's a tough question to answer, because it's hard to be objective about it. Ask a trusted friend or mentor for help.

Can a compromise be reached? Have you thought through all possible options? Perhaps there is a middle way both of you can accept. Do you know what you're doing? Can you live with the consequences of your choices?

I find it helpful to first compile a list of pros and cons of the decision you want to make, and the one your parents want you to make. Next, give each pro and each con a rating from one to ten depending on how important or significant it is to you, and see how it adds up. You should not necessarily base your decision on which side has the higher score, but this exercise gives you a clearer perspective of the overall costs and benefits of your options.

Throughout my schooling years my choices and what my mom want-ed differed, both in terms of choice of school and choice of subjects. My mom wanted the best for me, but she didn't know what I knew, or what I wanted (it's my fault – being an angsty teenager I didn't tell her). I was the best judge of that, so I made my own decisions. Lucky for me, my mom let go and gave me her support.

You will never know for sure whether you are making the right choice until you look back on it, perhaps many years down the road. Once you have made your choice, write down why you are making that choice. Here is part of what I wrote: "I have to make my decision and, at this point of time, with all the available information I have, this seems to be the wisest choice for both the short and long term future."

In the end it's your life, it's your choice, and you should make it.

Dream Killer #4 – Sneering Peers

"You can't do it, man. Wake up!" Sometimes your peers belittle you. Cruel words are their weapon of choice to sabotage your plans and dreams, and it feels like you've taken a torpedo in the side.

To keep afloat, distance yourself as far as you can from them. What if they're your friends? Ask yourself these questions: Was the cruel remark a one-off event uttered in a rash moment? Will they change if you tell them their words hurt?

If the answers to these questions are "no", they are just people you hang out with. You can choose your friends and whom you spend time with. Choose to stay away.

I know this is a hard thing for a young person to do, because friends are such a major part of your life. But if you believe in what you're doing, be brave and go it alone. Cherish the friends who believe in and encourage you.

Dream Killer #5 – Bad Luck

> People are always blaming their circumstances for what they are. I don't believe in circumstances. The people who get on in this world are the people who get up and look for the circumstances they want, and, if they can't find them, make them.
>
> – *George Bernard Shaw*

Bad things happen. You might have been making your way towards your dreams when an unfortunate twist of fate throws you off track. A serious injury, your prized guitar gets stolen or your computer crashes with all your data in it. You think to yourself: "It's over. All over."

Take some time off to get over the shock, then conduct a thorough inventory of your current situation: With what you have now, can you make your way back to where you were previously? What are your new limitations? How can you overcome them?

Dream Killer #6 – Lack of Resources

Let's say you can't sing or play any instruments, and yet your greatest desire is to record your own music album and become a pop star. Most people would tell you: "Dream on." A few might say to you, "Well, it depends on how badly you want it."

Sometimes there exists a large gap between the resources (talents, skills and materials) you have now and what you need to reach your goals.

To record an album you need to learn how to sing and probably how to play an instrument like the guitar or keyboard. If you plan to sing original compositions, you have to learn how to compose songs too. These are your intermediate goals. If you don't complete these steps, you will not be able to successfully reach your ultimate goal of recording your own album.

Sometimes you are hindered by your lack of resourcefulness. You do not have the know-how, the street smarts or the connections needed to proceed. Keep your eyes open to the possibilities. My three favourite methods of figuring out how to do anything are:

1.   The library. I don't want to sound melodramatic, but the library changed my life. When I couldn't figure something out, needed help to solve a problem or just wanted to find out more about a topic I was interested in, you'd find me there. Almost anything I wanted to know, the library had it. Absolutely free of charge (other than the fines I had to pay for all my late returns). I had four library cards to use – my mom's, my sister's, my brother's and mine. I would cart home large numbers of books. I was a bona fide nerd. The library was the portal through which I entered into a whole new world of awareness. Don't underestimate the possibilities there.

2. The Internet. Surpassing even the library in breadth of coverage is the Internet. Those of you who have grown up with the Internet will not realise what an incredible invention it is. It has greatly levelled the playing field, letting anyone with a computer and an Internet connection access amazing amounts of information. Though it cannot compare in terms of depth to a good book on the same subject, you will almost never fail to dig up something relevant to what you need to know.

3. Talks and courses. A great way to get the answers and skills you need, straight from the experts. Especially if you are planning to pick up a skill, save yourself potentially damaging mistakes and learn it from the people who've been there before. Whether you want to play the drums, swing dance or scuba dive, attending talks and courses is a good way to learn.

Surviving the onslaught

Dream Killers can be deadly but you are deadlier still because you now know how to overcome them. Taking action is the best road out of feelings of helplessness and incompetence. Don't know what to do? Look it up. Think it through. Do it.

MANAGING YOUR TIME

Where does all your time go? How are you using your time? If you're like most people you probably have no idea. When you fail to plan your day, the result is often a wasted day.

Don't get me wrong, once in a while we all need to take time off to goof and relax – only a control freak would sit down and plan out how he or she is going to bum. But for the majority of your days you have homework to do, tests to study for and goals you hope to achieve. And for those days when work needs to be done you have to plan your time to keep track and make the most of it.

Whatever your current level of personal efficiency, it can be further improved by using a system to match the time you have to the tasks you need to do. You've probably tried to set a schedule for yourself before and found it too difficult. Maybe you thought: "Oh it doesn't work for me, I just can't seem to follow it." While I can't say that setting a schedule will work for everyone (like the artistic types perhaps), I do know you've got to stick with it for the long haul to see results.

Don't worry about not being able to do everything on your schedule, it happens. Even now I'm at the stage where I can't find the discipline or energy to do up to 50% of the things I want to do in a day. But I know that if I didn't plan my time, that figure would be much closer to 0%.

Step 1 – Start with a monthly plan

You may already have one of these. Basically, it's a calendar for a particular month with lots of boxes on it. It tells you, at a glance, what you have in store for the coming month. If you don't have one, you can either make one yourself or download it for free from the Aktive Learning website (www.aktive.com.sg).

On this calendar put down all the appointments, test and exam dates, student group meetings, training sessions, school and public holidays, and courses you can think of. These are your responsibilities as a student, club member, volunteer or for whatever other roles you've taken on.

Back to our imaginary friend Joe. Whenever Joe gets new appointments, assignments or deadlines he adds it to his schedule. This month-at-a-glance chart gives him a broad perspective on how his month will go, and ensures he does not miss any important deadlines. It also helps him keep track of the progress he is making on his goals. Joe had previously figured out the date to organise the post-exam BBQ celebration for his classmates. He proceeds to fill in these dates in his monthly schedule:

May 2007

Mon	Tue	Wed	Thu	Fri	Sat	Sun
	1 Labour day	2 Sam's birthday	3 Soccer training, 4–6pm	4	5	6 Chinese tuition, 2–4pm
7	8 Soccer training, 4–6pm	9	10 Soccer training, 4–6pm	11	12	13 Chinese tuition, 2–4pm
14 Chinese test, 8–10am	15 English test, 8–10am	16 Mathematics test, 8–10am	17 Science test, 8–10am	18	19 Sharon's birthday party, 7–10pm	20 Chinese tuition, 2–4pm
21	22 Soccer training, 4–6pm	23 Post-exam BBQ, 6–10pm	24 Soccer training, 4–6pm	25	26	27 Chinese tuition, 2–4pm
28	29	30	31			

Step 2 – Create a daily/weekly schedule

From a broad monthly perspective, we now zero in on the details to figure out what you'll be doing from hour to hour. You can choose between doing a daily schedule or a weekly one. I personally find a daily schedule too time-consuming as my life is not so "eventful" (e.g. meeting at 8:15 A.M., video conference with client in Japan at 8:55 A.M. etc.) that I need to plan it in so much detail. It is also easier for you to fit a school timetable neatly into a weekly schedule.

Put all your class times and your student group and other outside commitments into your schedule. These are the events you have to attend. Next, schedule time to work on your goals – even just thirty minutes a day will make a big difference.

Don't overload your time by scheduling stuff back-to-back throughout the entire day. You should leave "gaps" in between for you to relax, make phone calls, surf the net or watch your favourite TV programme. We're not robots, and you'll frustrate yourself if you try to squeeze in too much.

Here's an example of a weekly schedule:

May 2007

	Mon 7	Tue 8	Wed 9	Thu 10	Fri 11	Sat 12	Sun 13
0800 0900	Mathematics	Chemistry	Literature	Mathematics	Chinese		Family time
1000	Recess						
1100 1200	History	Physics	Mathematics	Chemistry	Biology		
1300	Lunch						
1400 1500	Chinese	English	Biology	History	Physics	Swimming	Chinese tuition
1600 1700		Soccer		Soccer			
1800	Dinner						
1900 2000	Review and homework	Review and homework	Review and homework	Review and homework	Review and homework	Dinner and movie with friends	Review and homework
2100	Learn five new words and read Chinese news online						
2200							
2300	Sleep						

Keep track of how much time you really need for certain tasks, and adjust your schedule to make it more realistic. Often there's a discrepancy between how much time we think we need to do something and the time it actually takes. For example, I might schedule two hours to study one chapter of a textbook when in reality it takes four.

Also pay attention to your energy levels throughout the day – are you a morning person or a night person? Schedule the most demanding tasks during the period when you have the most energy and are most awake.

Every night before you sleep take five minutes to take stock of what tasks you have completed and to make changes to the next day's schedule if necessary.

Every week (Sunday evening is usually a good time to do this) spend fifteen minutes evaluating the progress you are making towards your goals and to plan the next week's schedule.

You're the boss

As you begin to manage your time you will learn more about your habits and preferences. Use that knowledge to make further changes to your own system.

I find it helps to keep your list of goals and weekly and monthly schedules all in one place for easy reference. Make it a habit to use the system. As you complete the tasks you have scheduled for yourself you can cancel them off. That's satisfying – you told yourself you were going to do something and you did it.

Don't be too hard on yourself if you didn't do something you planned to do. We all know how hard it is to put off a favourite TV show or a phone call to a friend and get to work. Procrastination is a problem that plagues not just students, but people of all ages.

Planning your life (your dreams, your goals and your time) helps you get things done so you have more time for fun. By controlling how you spend your time, you can confidently manoeuvre your way through life.

A BEAUTIFUL BEGINNING

Our Earth, the third planet from the sun, is but one of eight (it used to be nine, but Pluto got demoted) planets in our solar system, which is itself one of a million million stars in our galaxy (the Milky Way), which is one of the many galaxies in the universe. Each of us is but one out of more than six billion human beings on Earth.

Faced with these numbers it is easy to feel insignificant. Never mind the entire Earth – even within your own group of friends you may feel you don't matter, that if you disappeared tomorrow nobody would notice.

I can offer no magic formulas. That is the way the world is. Even without us, the world will go on. What I have found is that living a self-centred life is meaningless, but by reaching out and touching the lives of others, we can give our lives meaning. I imagine Mother Theresa would have been the most important person in the lives of the destitute sick and dying she served. Of course, that is an extreme example. Not all of us are called to make such a contribution.

In our own ways, whether it is to our family, to society or to the economy, we have much to contribute. Some people dedicate their lives to caring for the sick and aged. Others build great wealth to share it for everyone's benefit. As long as we leave this world better off than when we came into it, we have made a positive difference.

On a more personal level, expect less and give more to the people around you. Truly loving people live on in the memories of those who they have touched. Be someone wonderful to know.

Some people find meaning and answers to the big questions in life in their religious faith. Religion is a very sensitive issue, so I will tread carefully. What I believe is each individual must come to terms with his or her own faith. There are a lot of beliefs and "ways" out there. As you explore each one keep an open but sceptical mind.

> The unexamined life is not worth living
>
> *– Socrates*

Ask yourself the following and be patient with the answers, for at first it may feel like you've been thrown into a desert blindfolded in search of an oasis:

✦ **Why am I here?** Is there a reason for my existence? What is the meaning of my life? You might find your answer in a religion or a cause to fight for or in other people.

✦ **How am I going to live?** What principles am I going to live by? What truths do I hold sacred?

✦ **What is my idea of a successful life?** What does success mean to me? Is it having lots of money? Being famous? Climbing to the top of the corporate ladder? Having a happy family? Or just ruling the world? Essentially: what do I value?

✦ **What am I going to do now?** Am I going to be captain of my ship, or let random winds determine my bearing? Do I have a map to help me navigate? What, at this very moment, can I do to get closer to my chosen destination?

Some of the answers change as you grow older. Some questions do not have complete answers. The important thing is that you ask yourself these questions. Answer your questions, then question your answers.

I hope by asking and honestly answering these questions, you begin to see life in a new light, and you find more meaning in the way you you spend your time.

Change is possible

Recently a friend of mine asked: "Andrew, how come you're so motivated to do all these things?" And I thought to myself: Me? Motivated? Then it dawned on me that perhaps I've changed so gradually I never noticed it, that perhaps my little efforts have been paying off. And I get a kick out of thinking: "I'm improving! I'm getting better!" It's not true that a leopard can't change its spots. It's hard, but it can be done (even if it involves some cosmetic surgery).

I want to change. And what's helping me is the growing realisation that life is less and less about me and more and more about other people. From being self-centred I want to become more others-centred.

A life worth living

> It is not enough to be happy to have an excellent life. The point is to be happy while doing things that stretch our skills, that help us to grow and fulfil our potential. This is especially true in our early years: A teenager who feels happy doing nothing is unlikely to grow into a happy adult.
>
> — *Mihaly Csikszentmihalyi*

As kids, we were carefree. We lived in our own worlds. Like the proverbial frog in the well, we thought the patch of sky we could see was the whole world itself. But there is so much more.

When I was twenty this twenty-six year-old lady told me how envious she was of my youth. I remember feeling amused because twenty-six is still young by any standards, and she still had such a long way ahead, so much time to live and experience life. But then I thought: "Gosh, if only I knew what I know now when I was thirteen, if only I could go back and try it again, I could do so much more, learn so much more."

But whatever age you are now it's not too late. As long as you're alive it's never too late. Learn from your past mistakes. Use the emotion generated by regret with how you've spent your time in the past to propel yourself forward.

> Man needs difficulties. They are necessary for health.
> — *Carl Jung, Swiss psychiatrist*

Life is tough. It's unrealistic to expect it to be smooth sailing. There will be times when you feel down or depressed, when things are not going your way. There will be troubles and problems and challenges and obstacles. At times, life can be heart-wrenching and unbearable. It might seem happiness is merely a brief respite between periods of suffering. Don't give up. Weather it through, because no matter how painful it is, it will pass.

> It is said an Eastern monarch once charged his wise men to invent him a sentence to be ever in view and appropriate in all times and situations. They presented him the words, 'And this, too, shall pass away.' How much it expresses! How chastening in the hour of pride! How consoling in the depths of affliction.
>
> *— Abraham Lincoln*

Like you, I'm a fellow traveller on the same confusing journey. But I've seen a bit of the map, and I've learnt some things about the terrain. I'm the guy who says "Hey! Over here. I think I found a better way." What I hope to help you see is the bigger picture in your life. It's your life, and the choices are all yours to make.

By taking constructive action to achieve your goals and dreams, you can escape from the vicious cycle of boredom, depression and helplessness. Make good use of your time and youth now and you will have a much brighter future ahead. Sweat a bit more now and you'll be glad you did next time. You'll also appreciate more the life you've been given, and perhaps even create lifelong memories to reminisce about when your grandkids are sitting on your lap ("When grandpa was young...").

There's a path over here. Want to try it? I think it'll be fun.

EPILOGUE

Dear friend,

I hope this book has been entertaining as well as useful to you. Please let me know what you think of it or if you have any questions (or even to point out typos and mistakes!). You can contact me via email at andrew@aktive.com.sg.

Meanwhile don't forget to head to www.aktive.com.sg to sign up for my free newsletter where I'll be answering your questions and sending out interesting articles periodically. Also under the "Resources" section of the website you'll find lots of free useful stuff including blank forms to help you set goals and manage your time.

By making it this far in the book you have shown your desire and dedication to succeed in life. May your road ahead be filled with success, love and meaning.

Take care,
Andrew K. J. Tan

RECOMMENDED READS

The following books have positively influenced the way I live. You can find them in most bookstores or libraries.

Flow: The Psychology of Optimal Experience
Mihaly Csikszentmihalyi

Frames of Mind: The Theory of Multiple Intelligences
Howard Gardner

Notes from a Friend: A Quick and Simple Guide to Taking Control of Your Life
Anthony Robbins

Taking Responsibility: Self Reliance and the Accountable Life
Nathaniel Branden

The Road Less Traveled: A New Psychology of Love, Traditional Values and Spiritual Growth
M. Scott Peck

ABOUT THE AUTHOR

Andrew K. J. Tan was born and raised in Singapore, where he spent his first twenty years, before going on scholarship to Stanford University in Palo Alto, California. A top student and member of Phi Beta Kappa (the oldest American academic honours society), he earned a Bachelor in Economics (Distinction) along with a Master in Management Science and Engineering in four years.

While at Stanford he was selected to be head academic counsellor of a sixty-person dorm, and supervised a team of peer advisors. He also managed over forty tutors to provide subject tutoring for the entire undergraduate community.

At the age of twenty-four he became Site Director of the Stanford Asia Technology Initiative, where he helped set up the inaugural Global Entrepreneurship Conference in Singapore.

Andrew has written for *Teens Magazine* and is currently a fund manager at a global investment firm. In his spare time he loves to read, sing and dream.

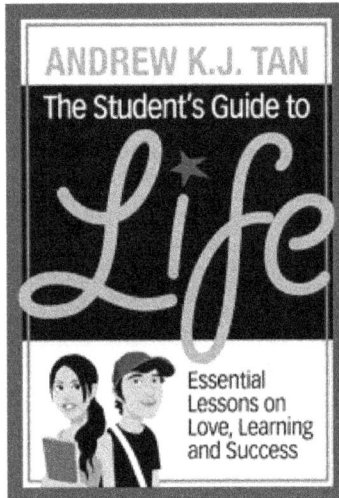

www.ingramcontent.com/pod-product-compliance
Lightning Source LLC
Chambersburg PA
CBHW031514040426
42445CB00009B/222